McDougal Littell Science

CALIFORNIA

Interactive
Reader

FOCUS ON LIFE SCIENCES

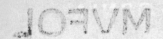

Focus on Life Sciences

Interactive Reader

Table of Contents

To the Student

The *Interactive Reader* makes reading science exciting. As you read, you can interact with this book. You can write in the book to help you remember what you have read.

Before each chapter, **The Big Idea** helps you understand what the chapter will be about. You can review ideas and words that you learned earlier. Use the preview activities to help you learn new words.

As you read each chapter:

- **Instant Replay** questions quickly check your understanding of what you read. You can write your answers on the page.

- **Mark It Up** boxes are near some of the pictures. These will help you draw a reminder about the concepts you have just learned.

- **Activity** reminders refer to activities and labs in the student text. They give you a fun way to do science.

- **Academic Vocabulary** words are defined at the bottom of some pages. These words occur in all subject areas.

- **Sample Calculations** show you how to use scientific formulas. You can follow the steps needed to solve a problem.

- **Visual Connections** refer to helpful pictures in your student text.

- **ClassZone.com** boxes tell you about more activities on the Internet.

At the end of each chapter, review what you have learned. Answer the questions about **vocabulary** and **key concepts.** Practice using your math skills. **The Big Idea** question reminds you about the main focus of each chapter. **Test Practice** questions help you become comfortable with multiple-choice science questions.

The *Interactive Reader* makes science fun and easier to understand!

the BIG idea

All living things are made up of cells.

Getting Ready to Learn

Review Concepts

- Living things share certain characteristics that make them different from nonliving things.

Activity

Cells
See student text, page 7.

Review Vocabulary

Draw a line to connect each word to its definition.

cell   a living thing

genetic material   the basic unit of life

organism   DNA

theory   a widely accepted scientific idea

Preview Key Vocabulary

For each pair of terms, explain what they have in common. Then, tell how they are different.

unicellular   multicellular

Similar: _____

Different: _____

prokaryotic cell   eukaryotic cell

Similar: _____

Different: _____

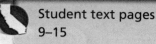

What makes living things different from nonliving things?

You know that a tree is alive but a rock is not. What exactly makes them different?

Characteristics of Life

An organism is a living thing. There are four main characteristics that all living things share.

1. **Organization** Living things have bodies and cells that are organized into different parts.

2. **Growth and development** Living things grow and usually develop into adult forms.

3. **Response to the environment** Living things respond to the world around them.

4. **Reproduction** Living things reproduce, or make new living things that are like themselves.

In the paragraph above, underline the four characteristics that living things share.

Needs of Life

Living things need energy, materials, and space. Plants get energy from the sun. Other living things eat plants as food. Food has the energy and materials that living things need to grow and reproduce.

What are three things that living things need to live?

Animals in this lake get energy and materials by eating food. Water provides living space.

_____ _____ _____

What is a cell?

A cell is the smallest unit* of a living thing. Some living things are made of one cell. Living things that are made of only one cell are called **unicellular.** Most unicellular living things are too small to see with just your eyes. The drawing below shows a unicellular organism much bigger than it really is.

Other living things are made of many cells. Living things that are made of more than one cell are **multicellular.** Most living things that are big enough to see are multicellular.

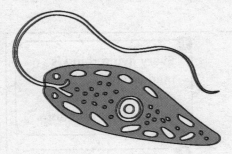

This organism is unicellular. It only has one cell.

This organism is multicellular. It has many cells.

The bodies of multicellular organisms—like you and the butterfly above—are made up of different types of cells.

 What type of organism are you—unicellular or multicellular? _____

What can a microscope do?

Most cells are too small to see with just your eyes. But cells can be seen with the help of a microscope. A **microscope** is a tool that makes something look bigger than it is.

 Why are microscopes so important to the study of cells?

_____

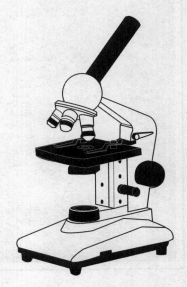

Microscopes allow people to see very small things.

*Academic Vocabulary: A **unit** is a basic, or elementary part, of something. A cell is the smallest **unit** of life because all life functions can happen in a cell.

Are all organisms made of cells?

People first saw cells more than 300 years ago with the help of microscopes. The discovery of cells led to many questions: Where do cells come from? Are all living things made of cells? Years of scientific work led to the cell theory, which answers these and other questions. There are three major parts of the **cell theory:**

1. Every living thing is made of one or more cells.
2. All cells carry out the functions needed for life.
3. New cells come only from other living cells.

1. **Every living thing is made of one or more cells.** This polar bear is a multicellular organism.

2. **Cells carry out the functions needed for life.** Fat cells help keep the bear warm.

3. **Cells come only from other living cells.** A new fat cell can grow from a single cell.

Fat Cells

 What part of cell theory describes the main role of cells? Underline the sentence that tells you.

How did the cell theory change biology?

A scientific theory is a widely accepted explanation of something in the natural world. Scientific theories, such as the cell theory, are very important because they describe our understanding of the natural world.

 What is a scientific theory ? _____

_____

The ideas of the cell theory changed the way scientists study biology. Scientists began to study cells. They found that there are single-celled organisms in the air, water, soil—everywhere! Many of these tiny single-celled organisms are **bacteria** (bak-TEER-ee-uh).

The study of cells led biology in a new direction. Scientists learned about many different ways that bacteria affect our lives. For example, they found that some bacteria can cause disease. They also found ways of stopping some of these diseases.

Have you ever smelled spoiled milk? Bacteria cause milk to spoil.

 What are bacteria? _____

_____

SECTION 1.1	
SUMMARIZE	**VOCABULARY**
1. What are the four main characteristics that all living things share? _____ _____ _____ _____ _____	Fill in each blank with the correct word. **unicellular multicellular microscope** **2.** Bacteria are _____ organisms. **3.** A _____ can be used to see cells. **4.** A bird is a _____ organism.

SECTION 1.2

Key Concept

Microscopes allow us to see inside the cell.

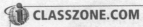

Student text pages 18–24

What can you see with a microscope?

There are different kinds of microscopes. Light microscopes can be used to see living cells. They can make things look up to one thousand times larger than they are.

Other types of microscopes are even more powerful. They can make things look one million times larger than they are! These types of microscopes are not used to study cells that are still alive.

 What kind of microscopes can be used to see living cells? _____

> **CLASSZONE.COM**
>
> **Visualization** View cells through different types of microscopes.

What do cells look like?

A cell is surrounded by a **cell membrane.** Anything that moves into or out of the cell must pass through the cell membrane. Inside of the membrane is the **cytoplasm** (SY-tuh-PLAZ-uhm). The cytoplasm is a thick liquid material.

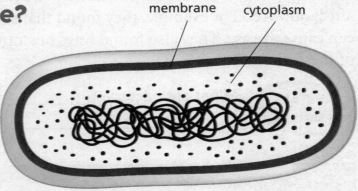

membrane   cytoplasm

Cells have a membrane and cytoplasm.

 Fill in the blanks: The _____ surrounds a cell. Inside of the cell is the _____.

Two Types of Cells

There are two main types of cells—prokaryotic cells and eukaryotic cells. You can tell them apart by looking at them.

1. In **prokaryotic cells** (proh-KAR-ee-AWT-ihk), the genetic material is in the cytoplasm. The picture shows this type of cell. Most unicellular organisms are prokaryotic cells.

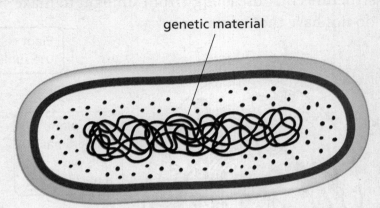

genetic material

You can tell that this is a prokaryotic cell because its genetic material is floating in the cytoplasm.

2. **Eukaryotic cells** (yoo-KAR-ee-AHT-ihk) have a nucleus. A **nucleus** (NOO-klee-uhs) is a membrane that surrounds and contains the cell's genetic material. Some other parts of eukaryotic cells are also surrounded by membranes. Any part within a cell that has a membrane around it and carries out a specialized job is called an **organelle** (AWR-guh-NEHL). Most multicellular organisms are made up of eukaryotic cells.

What is contained in a cell's nucleus? Underline the sentence that tells you.

What kind of cells make up plants and animals?

Plants and animals have eukaryotic cells. Like other eukaryotic cells, plant and animal cells have cell membranes, cytoplasm, and nuclei.*

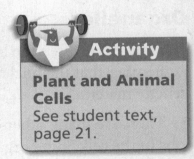

Activity

Plant and Animal Cells
See student text, page 21.

*Academic Vocabulary: **Nuclei** is the plural form of the word *nucleus.*

Plant and animal cells are different in several ways. For example, plant cells have a **cell wall** that surrounds the cell membrane. The cell wall is firm and holds the shape of the plant cell. Plant cells also have structures that use energy from sunlight to make sugars. Animal cells do not have these structures.

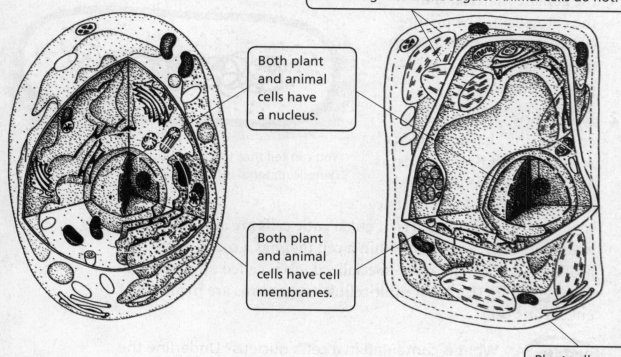

Plant cells have structures that enable them to use sunlight to make sugars. Animal cells do not.

Both plant and animal cells have a nucleus.

Both plant and animal cells have cell membranes.

Plant cells have a cell wall. Animal cells do not.

Which type of cell has a cell wall—a plant cell or an animal cell? _____

Organelles

The nucleus is often the largest organelle in a cell. Remember that the nucleus contains the cell's genetic material.

There are many other organelles that have different jobs in the cell. Some organelles use genetic information to make important molecules that the cell needs. Some organelles help cells to get energy. Other organelles store and move materials in the cell.

Mark It Up

Circle the nucleus in each cell.

Visual Connection

See Parts of a Eukaryotic Cell in the student text, page 22.

Two important organelles are chloroplasts and mitochondria. Both of these organelles help cells to get energy they need to live.

1. **Chloroplasts** (KLAWR-uh-PLASTS) are organelles that use the energy from sunlight to make sugars. The cell can then use the sugars as food. Most plant cells have chloroplasts, but animal cells do not.

2. **Mitochondria** (MY-tuh-KAHN-dree-uh) use oxygen and food to get energy for the cell to use. Both plant and animal cells have mitochondria. In plants, the mitochondria get energy from the sugars that are made in the chloroplasts. In animals, the mitochondria get energy from the food the animal eats.

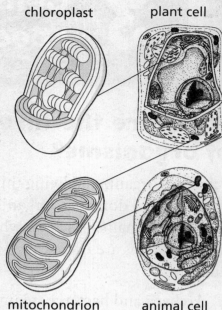

chloroplast   plant cell

mitochondrion   animal cell

Both plant and animal cells have mitochondria, but only plant cells have chloroplasts.

Fill in the blanks: Both plant and animal cells have organelles called _____. Plant cells, but not animal cells, have _____.

SECTION 1.2	
SUMMARIZE	**VOCABULARY**
1. What are two things that eukaryotic cells have but prokaryotic cells do not? _____ _____ _____ _____ _____	2. Circle the names of the cell parts that are found in both plant and animal cells. cell membrane cytoplasm mitochondria nucleus cell wall chloroplast

Student text pages 26–32

What are the three major groups of organisms?

Scientists organize all living things into three major groups called domains. Organisms are put into one of the three domains based on what their cells are like. The three domains are Archaea (AHR-kee-uh), Bacteria, and Eukarya.

Activity

Specialization
See student text, page 26.

Archaea and bacteria are unicellular organisms. Archaea and bacteria are all prokaryotic cells. Bacteria look like Archaea but they are in their own domain because they have genetic differences.

Circle the word that completes each sentence:
Archaea and bacteria are **prokaryotic / eukaryotic** cells.
They are **multicellular / unicellular.**

The domain Eukarya includes organisms with eukaryotic cells. Recall from Section 1.2 that a eukaryotic cell has a nucleus. There are many single-celled organisms in this domain. Almost all multicellular organisms are in this domain.

Fill in the blank: All eukaryotic organisms are in the domain _____.

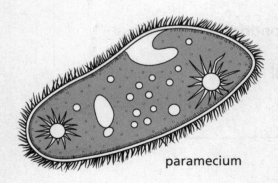

paramecium

lizard

The domain Eukarya includes both unicellular and multicellular organisms.

What makes multicellular organisms have different types of cells?

Most multicellular organisms have many different types of cells. The different types of cells are specialized to do different jobs. **Specialization** means that only some types of cells can carry out specific functions* in the organism.

For example, most animals have blood cells, nerve cells, and muscle cells. You can see each of these types of cells in the drawing. Each of these types of cells has different functions. Some blood cells carry oxygen. Other blood cell types can help you fight an infection. Nerve cells take signals to other cells, and muscle cells move the organism. Just as they have different functions, these cells also have different shapes.

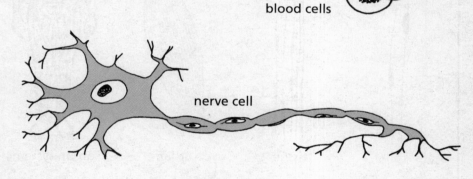

blood cells

The different specialized cells cannot live outside of the multicellular organisms they belong to. For example, a single leaf cell or blood cell cannot survive apart from the whole organism. Different specialized cells all work together to keep an organism alive.

nerve cell

The cells of multicellular organisms are specialized to do different jobs.

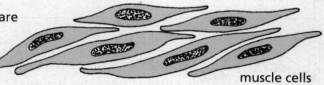

muscle cells

INSTANT REPLAY

Which type of organism has specialized cells, a unicellular organism or a multicellular organism?

_____

*Academic Vocabulary: **Function** means job or task. The **function** of your pencil is to allow you to write.

What are the different levels of organization in a multicellular organism?

Plants and animals are more than just big blobs of cells. Many cells work together to form a **tissue.** Many tissues work together to form an **organ.** Many organs work together to form an organ system. And all of the organ systems work together to form an organism. These levels of organization are shown below.

Visual Connection
See Levels of Organization in the student text, page 30.

Levels of Organization

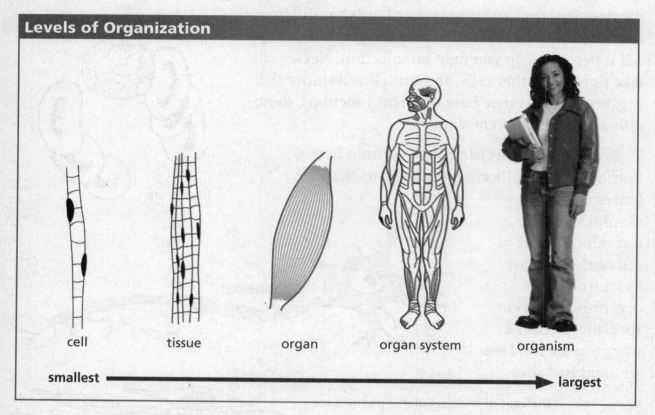

cell   tissue   organ   organ system   organism

smallest ➤ largest

Look at the drawings. Which level of organization is the highest, or biggest? _____

What kinds of models do scientists use to study cells?

Scientists use models to study cells. There are many different types of models. The drawings of cells in this book are one kind of model. Computer models are also important tools scientists use to help understand cells.

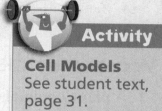

Activity

Cell Models
See student text, page 31.

What are two examples of models?

_____ _____

SECTION 1.3	
SUMMARIZE	**VOCABULARY**
1. How are tissues different from organs?	Draw a line to connect each word with its definition.
_____ _____ _____ _____ _____ _____	2. **specialization** a. group of cells that work together 3. **tissue** b. cells with different shapes do different jobs 4. **organ** c. group of tissues that work together

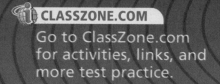
CLASSZONE.COM
Go to ClassZone.com
for activities, links, and
more test practice.

Vocabulary Circle the word that completes each sentence.

1 A **plant / animal** cell has a cell wall and chloroplasts.

2 The cells of multicellular organisms are **bacteria / specialized**.

3 In plant and animal cells, genetic information is contained in
the **cell membrane / nucleus**.

4 A group of cells that does a specific job is called a(n) **tissue / organ**.

Reviewing Key Concepts

5 Put the following terms in order from lowest level of
organization to highest level of organization: *organ system,
tissue, organism, cell, organ.*

_____

6 What are three parts of the cell theory?

_____

_____

_____

the BIG idea

7 How are unicellular organisms and multicellular organisms
similar? How are they different?

Similar: _____

Different: _____

Test Practice

8 Which of the following structures
are found in plant cells but not
animal cells?

   A nucleus

   B chloroplast

   C mitochondria

   D cell membrane

9 Unlike a eukaryotic cell, a
prokaryotic cell does not have

   A genetic material

   B a cell membrane

   C a nucleus

   D cytoplasm

2 How Cells Function

the BIG idea

All cells need energy and materials for life processes.

Getting Ready to Learn

Review Concepts

- Cells are the basic units of living things.
- Some cells have organelles that perform special functions for the cell.
- Animal cells and plant cells have similar structures, but only plant cells have cell walls and chloroplasts.

Activity

Photosynthesis
See student text, page 39.

Review Vocabulary

Write the correct term for each description.

organelle   **chloroplast**   **mitochondria**

Any part of a cell that is surrounded by a membrane and carries out a specialized function _____

Found in plant cells but not animal cells _____

Found in both plant cells and animal cells _____

Preview Key Vocabulary

Here are some terms you will learn in this chapter. As you read the chapter, write a sentence to explain how the terms are related. Write your sentences below.

Chlorophyll _____ photosynthesis.

Diffusion _____ osmosis.

Genetic material _____ nucleic acids.

Student text pages 41–45

Which elements make up cells?

Plants, animals, and bacteria are all made of the same elements. An element is a type of atom that has its own special characteristics. Hydrogen and oxygen are two kinds of elements.

More than a hundred different elements exist, but only about 25 of those are needed for life. In fact, all cells are made up of these same 25 elements. Look at the chart. Almost the entire human body is made up of only 6 elements: oxygen, carbon, hydrogen, nitrogen, calcium, and phosphorous.

Elements in the Human Body	
Oxygen	65.0%
Carbon	18.5%
Hydrogen	9.5%
Nitrogen	3.3%
Calcium	1.5%
Phosphorus	1.0%
other 19 elements	1.2%

Source: CRC Handbook of Chemistry and Physics

Mark It Up

Circle the element that makes up most of the human body.

Look at the chart above. Which three elements make up most of the human body?

_____ _____ _____

Molecules

The atoms of elements are not found alone. They are joined together with other atoms to form molecules.

Two of the same kind of atom may be joined together. For example, two oxygen atoms may be joined together to form a molecule of oxygen gas (O_2). Different kinds of atoms may also join together. For example, two hydrogen atoms joined with one oxygen atom form water (H_2O).

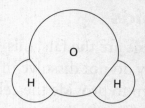

One molecule of water contains two hydrogen atoms and one oxygen atom.

 Which two elements make up a water molecule?

_____   _____

Chemical Reactions

Cells have different parts, such as organelles, cell membranes, and genetic material. All of the parts of the cell are made up of molecules. Atoms and molecules interact inside cells.

Some interactions are chemical reactions. A **chemical reaction** is a process in which bonds* between atoms are broken or new bonds are formed. When bonds are broken, a molecule is taken apart. When bonds are formed, new atoms are added to a molecule.

 What happens in a chemical reaction? Underline the sentence above that tells you.

Which large molecules are found in cells?

There are four types of large molecules in living things: carbohydrates, lipids, proteins, and nucleic acids. Each type of molecule plays important roles in the cell. The different molecules all work together to carry out cell functions.

Carbohydrates

A **carbohydrate** (KAHR-boh-HY-DRAYT) is made up of sugars that are linked together. Carbohydrates may be broken down to provide the cell with energy. Other carbohydrates are part of cell structure. For example, they make up plant cell walls.

Carbohydrates provide structure and store energy in cells.

*Academic Vocabulary: A **bond** holds two things together. You like to be around your friend, and so the two of you have a **bond**.

Lipids

Lipids are the fats, oils, and waxes found in living things. They do not dissolve in water. Lipids may be broken down to provide the cell with energy. Other lipids are part of cell structure. For example, they form the membranes around cells and organelles.

Fats and oils are lipids, and they do not dissolve in water.

 Which type of molecule is a main part of cell membranes? _____

Proteins

Proteins are made of smaller molecules called amino acids. There are many different types of proteins with many different functions. Proteins are important for chemical reactions, cell growth and repair, fighting infections, cell membranes, and many other structures and activities.

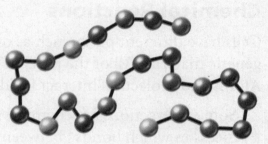

Proteins are made up of amino acids.

Nucleic acids

Nucleic acids (noo-KLEE-ihk) hold the instructions for cells to develop, grow, and reproduce. Nucleic acids are molecules that form genetic material—DNA and RNA.

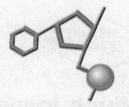

Nucleic acids hold the cell's genetic information.

 Which type of molecule holds a cell's genetic information? _____

Large Molecule Summary Chart	
Type of Molecule	**Function in Cells**
Carbohydrate	structure and energy
Lipid	
Protein	many different functions
Nucleic acid	

Mark It Up

Fill in the blank boxes in the chart.

All cells contain carbohydrates, lipids, proteins, and nucleic acids. In all cells, each type of molecule has similar functions. For example, all cells have membranes that are made mostly of lipids. All cells have genetic material made up of nucleic acids. The cells of all living things function similarly.

 What is one example of how all cells function similarly?

How much of a cell is made of water?

Most of a cell—about 70 percent—is water. Many materials dissolve in water. The chemical reactions of life take place in the water inside and outside of cells.

Most lipids—fats and oils—do not dissolve in water. A special kind of lipid makes up cell membranes. This type of lipid, shown to the left, has two parts: the "head" of the lipid is attracted to water. The "tails" keep away from water.

Activity

Oil and Water
See student text, page 44.

Mark It Up

Color the part of the molecule that is attracted to water blue. Color the part that keeps away from water red.

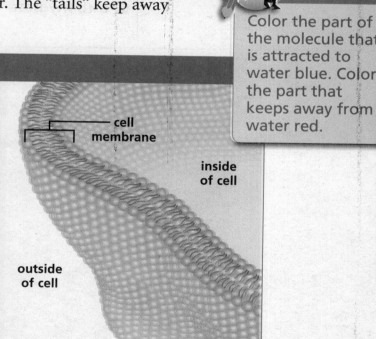

Cell Membrane

The cell membrane is made of a double layer of lipids.

Many lipid molecules make up the cell membrane.

head

tails

cell membrane

inside of cell

outside of cell

Look at the drawing of a cell membrane again. It shows that the cell membrane is made of two layers of lipid molecules. The heads of the lipids point away from each other. One side faces the inside of the cell. The other side faces the outside of the cell. The tails face each other.

 How many layers of lipids make up the cell membrane?

_____

SECTION 2.1

SUMMARIZE	VOCABULARY
1. What are four types of large molecules that are common to all cells? _____ _____ _____ _____	Draw a line to connect each word to its definition. **2. chemical reaction** **a.** makes up cell membranes **3. lipid** **b.** can be broken down for energy **4. nucleic acid** **c.** breaks apart some molecules or makes new ones **5. carbohydrate** **d.** makes up the cell's genetic material

SECTION

2.2

Key Concept

Cells capture and release energy.

Student text pages
47–54

What kind of energy do cells use?

All cells use chemical energy to stay alive. **Chemical energy** is the energy stored in the bonds between atoms of every molecule. All cells must release the chemical energy stored in bonds to stay alive.

A major energy source for all cells is glucose. **Glucose** is a sugar molecule. Cells release chemical energy stored in glucose molecules. Your cells use energy when you run, walk, and even sleep. Your cells always need energy.

Your cells release chemical energy from food. If you need more energy, you eat more food. Plants do not get their glucose by eating. Plants use the energy from sunlight to make glucose and other sugars.

How is the way an animal gets glucose different from the way a plant gets glucose?

_____

_____

_____

_____

_____

When you eat food, you get energy. The energy in the wheat bread originally came from the sun.

How do plant cells capture light energy?

Photosynthesis (FOH-toh-SIHN-thih-sihs) is the process that plant cells use to change the energy in sunlight into the chemical energy in glucose.

Visual Connection
See Photosynthesis in the student text, page 49.

Photosynthesis takes place in plant cells that have organelles called chloroplasts. Chloroplasts contain a substance called chlorophyll (KLAWR-uh-fihl). **Chlorophyll** is a molecule that captures* the energy in sunlight.

 Where is chlorophyll found? _____

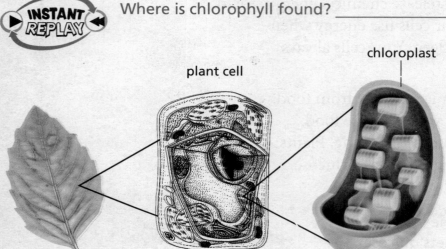

plant cell

chloroplast

Chloroplasts capture energy from sunlight for photosynthesis.

 In what organelle does photosynthesis take place? _____
What molecule in this organelle captures the energy in sunlight? _____

Mark It Up

Chlorophyll is not shown in these pictures. Circle the organelle in which chlorophyll is found.

*Academic Vocabulary: To **capture** something means to trap or catch it. You can **capture** a butterfly by trapping it in a net.

Plants make glucose and other sugars through photosynthesis. Plant cells then use the glucose for energy. Plants can also store* some of the glucose they make in their cells. Before plants can store glucose, they put many glucose molecules together. Long molecules with many glucose molecules in them are called starches.

The sugars and starches that plants make are also used by animals. When animals eat plants, they get the plants' sugars. These sugars give animals the energy their cells need. Other animals get sugars by eating other animals that already ate plants.

When you eat food, you are eating stored energy that came from photosynthesis.

What process do plant cells use to change the energy in sunlight into the chemical energy in glucose?

_____

How do cells use the energy stored in glucose?

All cells need energy. Cells get chemical energy from the bonds in glucose molecules. When cells break down glucose, they can use the energy that is released.

There are two basic processes that cells can use to break down glucose for energy: cellular respiration and fermentation. Cellular respiration requires oxygen, but fermentation does not. Cellular respiration releases much more energy than does fermentation.

What are two processes that cells use to release energy from glucose?

_____   _____

*Academic Vocabulary: To **store** something means to save it or keep it for later use. You might **store** food in a cabinet until you are ready to eat it.

Cellular Respiration

Plant and animal cells release energy from glucose during cellular respiration. **Cellular respiration** is a process in which cells use oxygen to release energy stored in glucose molecules. Cellular respiration occurs in organelles called mitochondria.

Visual Connection
See Cellular Respiration in the student text, page 49.

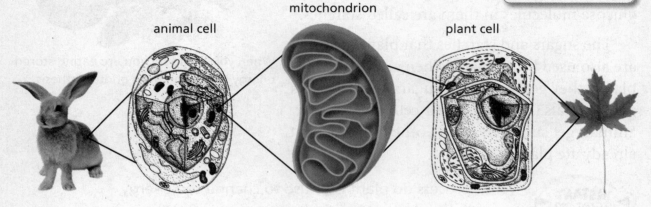

mitochondrion

animal cell

plant cell

Mitochondria release the energy in glucose through the process of cellular respiration.

In which organelle does cellular respiration occur?

_____

Fermentation

During **fermentation** cells release energy without using oxygen. The process of fermentation happens in the cytoplasm, not in the mitochondria. Fermentation releases much less energy than cellular respiration. The process of fermentation is important for some foods. Bread, yogurt, and cheese all use fermentation.

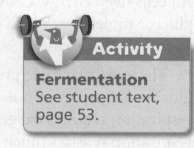

Activity

Fermentation
See student text, page 53.

What are two differences between fermentation and cellular respiration?

_____

_____

Energy and Exercise

Your muscle cells use both cellular respiration and fermentation to release energy. While oxygen is available, your muscle cells use cellular respiration. But during hard exercise, the oxygen can get used up. Without oxygen, your muscle cells use fermentation to release energy. Fermentation produces a waste product called lactic acid. This is what makes your muscles sore after hard exercise.

 Fill in the blanks: When there is oxygen available, your muscle cells use _____ to release energy. Without oxygen, muscle cells use _____.

SECTION 2.2	
SUMMARIZE	**VOCABULARY**
1. How do both photosynthesis and cellular respiration allow your cells to get the energy they need to live? _____ _____ _____ _____ _____ _____	Circle the word or phrase that makes each sentence correct. **2.** Cells produce more chemical energy through **cellular respiration / fermentation.** **3.** The process of **photosynthesis / cellular respiration** transforms the energy in sunlight into chemical energy. **4.** The process of **photosynthesis / cellular respiration** releases the energy stored in the bonds of glucose and other sugars.

Student text pages 56–63

How do materials get into and out of cells?

All cells need materials to live. Before a cell can use these materials, they must get into the cell. Some materials get into a cell by diffusion.

Diffusion (dih-FYOO-zhuhn) is the process by which molecules spread out. In diffusion, molecules move from areas where there are many of them to areas where there are fewer of them. The drawings below show one example of diffusion.

Activity

Diffusion
See student text, page 56.

Diffusion

A sugar cube dissolving in water provides an example of diffusion.

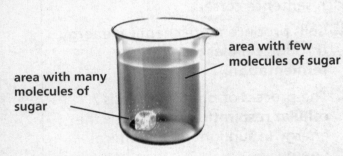

area with few molecules of sugar

area with many molecules of sugar

equal amount of sugar molecules throughout

1 Right after a sugar cube is put into a glass of water, most of the sugar molecules are in the same place, near the sugar cube.

2 Over time, diffusion causes the amount of sugar molecules to become the same all through the glass of water.

INSTANT REPLAY

Circle the word that makes each sentence correct: When molecules move by diffusion, they move from areas with **more** / **less** molecules to areas with **more** / **less** molecules.

Some molecules can diffuse directly across the cell membrane. For example, small molecules such as oxygen can pass through the cell membrane by diffusion. Some larger molecules, such as glucose, can pass through special passages in the cell membrane.

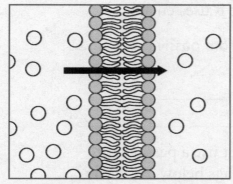

Some molecules can diffuse across the cell membrane.

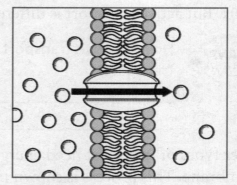

Other molecules can diffuse through special passages in the cell membrane.

When molecules diffuse through the membrane or through special passages in the membrane, the cell does not use any energy. Scientists use the term **passive transport** to describe the movement of materials that does not use the cell's energy.

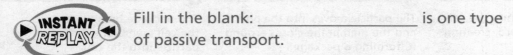

Fill in the blank: _____ is one type of passive transport.

Water molecules also move into and out of cells by diffusion. When water molecules move through a membrane, it is called **osmosis** (ahz-MOH-sihs). If there are more molecules of water outside of a cell than inside, the water molecules will move into the cell. If there are more water molecules inside the cell than outside, the water molecules will move out.

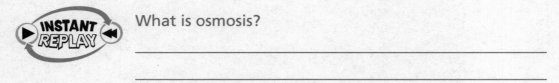

What is osmosis?

_____

_____

What kinds of transport require energy?

Active transport is the process of using energy to move materials through a membrane. In active transport, molecules move through a passage in the cell membrane. This is almost the same as passive transport. But active transport is different, because it uses energy.

 How is active transport different from passive transport?

_____

_____

Other types of transport need energy but do not use a passage in the membrane. This process is shown in the drawings below. Here you can see that this process can move large molecules out of cells.

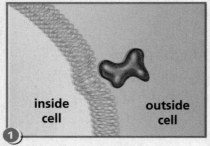

inside cell **outside cell**

① As a particle approaches, the cell membrane folds inward, creating a pocket.

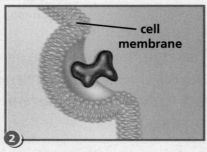

cell membrane

② The particle moves into the pocket, and the membrane closes around it, forming a package.

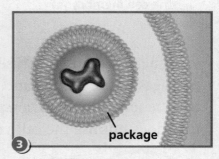

package

③ The package breaks away from the cell membrane, bringing the particle into the cell.

 What type of transport is shown in the drawings above, active transport or passive transport?

_____

How does cell size affect transport?

Cells are very small. Most are too small to be seen without a microscope. Smaller cells can move materials into and out of the cell more efficiently.* The shape of cells also affects the amount of materials that can be moved into or out of the cell.

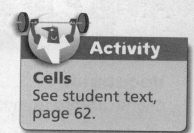

Activity

Cells
See student text, page 62.

What do cell size and shape affect?

_____

_____

SECTION 2.3	
SUMMARIZE	**VOCABULARY**
1. How is the energy needed for active transport different from the energy needed for passive transport? _____ _____ _____ _____ _____ _____	Fill in the blanks with the correct word. **active transport diffusion** **passive transport** Osmosis and other types of 2. _____ are examples of 3. _____. Large molecules move into and out of a cell by 4. _____.

*Academic Vocabulary: **Efficient** means effective, or works well. You do your homework **efficiently** when you do not waste time and your answers are correct.

Review
CHAPTER
2 How Cells Function

CLASSZONE.COM
Go to ClassZone.com for activities, links, and more test practice.

Vocabulary

Choose a word from the box, and write it next to its definition.

1 Process that captures light energy _____

2 Molecule that makes up cell membranes

   _____

3 Process that releases energy from glucose

   _____

4 Diffusion of water across a membrane _____

| cellular respiration |
| photosynthesis |
| lipid |
| osmosis |

Reviewing Key Concepts

5 Four large molecules that are important to the function of all cells are _____, _____, _____, and _____.

6 Osmosis and diffusion are two types of _____ transport.

the **BIG** idea

7 Describe how the processes of photosynthesis and cellular respiration get energy that cells can use.

   Photosynthesis: _____

   Cellular respiration: _____

Test Practice

8 Which type(s) of cells use cellular respiration?

   A plant cells only
   B animal cells only
   C both plant and animal cells
   D neither plant nor animal cells

9 Which of the following is a cellular process that releases energy that a cell can use?

   A osmosis
   B cellular respiration
   C active transport
   D photosynthesis

3 Cell Division

the BIG idea

Organisms grow, reproduce, and maintain themselves through cell division.

Getting Ready to Learn

Review Concepts

- The cell is the basic unit of life.
- All cells come from other cells.
- DNA provides the instructions a cell needs to function and reproduce.

Activity

Division and Volume
See student text, page 71.

Review Vocabulary

Draw a line to connect each word to the picture that it matches.

cell membrane   **nucleus**   **cycle**

 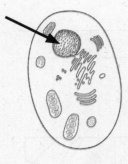 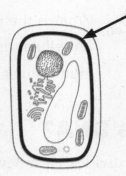

Preview Key Vocabulary

As you read the chapter, use the frames below to write important details about each of the terms.

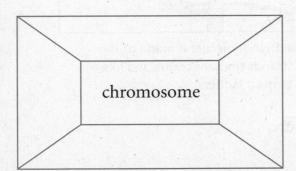

chromosome

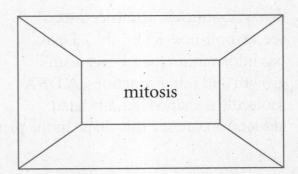

mitosis

Student text pages
73–78

What are the functions of cell division?

Cell division is a process that divides one cell into two cells. The process of cell division occurs in all organisms. There are several different functions of cell division.

Unicellular organisms A **unicellular organism** is made up of just one cell. When a unicellular organism divides into two cells, it reproduces. In other words, it produces offspring.

Multicellular organisms Most organisms that are big enough to be seen are **multicellular organisms**—they are made of more than one cell. Cell division helps multicellular organisms grow, develop, repair themselves, and reproduce.

What is the role of cell division in

unicellular organisms? _____

multicellular organisms? _____

What is DNA?

When a cell divides, each new cell needs a full copy of genetic material. The genetic material in cells is made up of DNA molecules.

   DNA is the genetic material in cells. The letters DNA stand for deoxyribonucleic acid (dee-AHK-see-RY-boh-noo-KLEE-ihk). DNA has information for an organism's growth and other functions. A DNA molecule is shaped like a twisted ladder. You can see this shape in the picture.

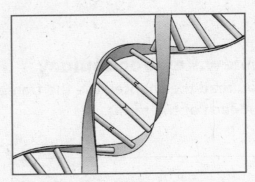

A DNA molecule is made of two strands that are connected like a twisted ladder.

What are chromosomes?

In a eukaryotic cell, most of the DNA is in the nucleus. When in the nucleus, DNA looks like long loose strands— like a plate of spaghetti. But before the cell divides, the DNA gets replicated, or copied. Then, it gets folded into compact* structures called **chromosomes** (KROH-muh-SOHMZ).

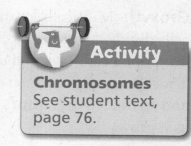

Activity

Chromosomes
See student text, page 76.

Remember that before a cell divides, the chromosomes get copied. The chromosome in the picture has two copies. This chromosome's right and left halves are held together in the center. The right and left parts are identical; they are copies of each other.

Remember that chromosomes are made up of DNA. But in the picture, the DNA strands are so small and tightly folded you cannot actually see them.

 How are chromosomes and DNA related?

_____

Each type of organism has a particular number of chromosomes. Humans have 46 chromosomes. Fern plants may have more than 100 chromosomes. Fruit flies only have 8.

 How many chromosomes do humans have?

_____

A chromosome is made of tightly packed DNA.

What is the role of cell division in growth, development, and repair?

You started out as one cell. How did you get so big? Your cells divided over and over. In multicellular organisms—including you—cell division is used for growth, development, and repair.

---

*Academic Vocabulary: **Compact** means small and tightly packed together. When you cram your clothes into a suitcase, the clothes are **compact**.

Growth Multicellular organisms grow as their cells divide. Most multicellular organisms start out as one cell. That cell divides into two cells. Those two cells can then divide into four cells, and so on. An organism's cells continue to divide as it grows.

Development As an organism grows, the cells do not look the same. During development, cells become specialized* to do different jobs. Some cells become skin cells and others become nerve cells. The different cells all have the same set of DNA, but they each do only one job.

Repair If you get a cut, your body uses cell division to repair itself. The surrounding cells divide and replace the damaged ones. Cell division also replaces cells that are old or worn out. Even after you are fully grown, your body will still use cell division to replace damaged cells.

This infant will grow as its cells divide.

 Circle three roles of cell division.

Visual Connection
See Repair in the student text, page 78.

SECTION 3.1	
SUMMARIZE	**VOCABULARY**
1. What are three main jobs of cell division in multicellular organisms? _____ _____ _____ _____ _____	Fill in each blank with the correct word from the list. **chromosomes** **DNA** **nucleus** In eukaryotic cells, the genetic material is contained in the **2.** _____. Before cell division, the genetic material, or **3.** _____, becomes tightly packaged into structures called **4.** _____.

*Academic Vocabulary: **Specialized** means only doing one job. The actors, set designers, and lighting experts each have **specialized** roles in the school play.

What is the cell cycle?

A cycle is a process that repeats. In the life cycle, living things grow, reproduce, and die. Cells have a life cycle too. A cell's life cycle is called the cell cycle. The **cell cycle** is the normal pattern of development and division of a cell. There are two main parts of the cell cycle: interphase and cell division.

Interphase As you can see in the picture, most of the cell's life cycle is spent in interphase. **Interphase** is the part of the cell cycle when the cell grows and carries out normal functions. The cell does not divide during interphase. But the cell gets ready to divide by copying, or replicating, its DNA.

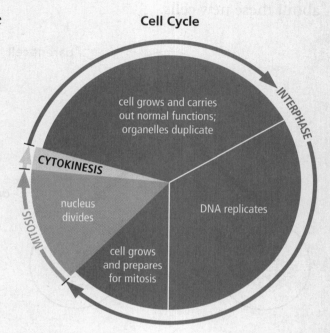

Cell Cycle

- cell grows and carries out normal functions; organelles duplicate
- INTERPHASE
- DNA replicates
- cell grows and prepares for mitosis
- MITOSIS
- nucleus divides
- CYTOKINESIS

Cell Division There are two parts of cell division: mitosis and cytokinesis.

- **Mitosis** is the process that divides the nucleus in eukaryotic cells. Remember that the nucleus holds a cell's DNA. The nucleus divides during mitosis. The cell's genetic material divides too.

- **Cytokinesis** (SY-toh-kuh-NEE-sihs) is the division of the cytoplasm.

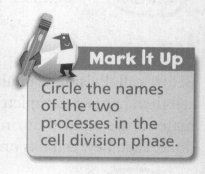

Mark It Up

Circle the names of the two processes in the cell division phase.

When mitosis and cytokinesis are done, there are two new cells. Each new cell has a complete set of DNA and other cell structures.

INSTANT REPLAY

What happens during mitosis?

_____

What are the products of cell division?

When a cell divides, it produces two new genetically identical*
cells. The cell that divides is called a parent cell. The two cells
that result are called daughter cells. The term *daughter cell* does
not mean that it's a female. It is just a term scientists use to talk
about these new cells.

Visual Connection
See Cell Division in
the student text,
page 83.

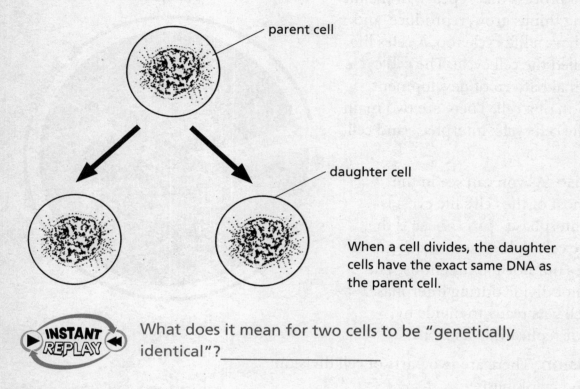

parent cell

daughter cell

When a cell divides, the daughter
cells have the exact same DNA as
the parent cell.

INSTANT REPLAY What does it mean for two cells to be "genetically
identical"?_____

Mitosis

Before cell division can take place, a parent cell's DNA is copied. The
cell then has two complete sets of DNA. The two copies of the genetic
material are divided during mitosis. This means that when mitosis is
done, each new cell has only one complete set of DNA.

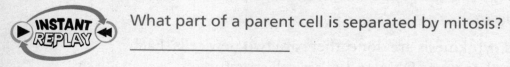

What part of a parent cell is separated by mitosis?
_____

*Academic Vocabulary: **Identical** means exactly the same. The pieces of blank paper in your
notebook are **identical** to one another.

Mitosis is a continuous process. It does not really happen in separate steps. However, it can be helpful to break the process into parts in order to learn about it. In general, mitosis happens in this way:

① CLASSZONE.COM

Visualization Watch the process of mitosis in action.

① DNA folds and forms chromosomes.

② Chromosomes line up.

③ Chromosomes separate.

④ New cells form during cytokinesis.

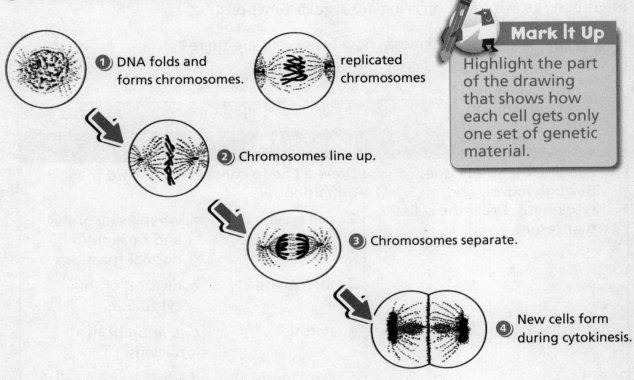

① DNA folds and forms chromosomes.

replicated chromosomes

② Chromosomes line up.

③ Chromosomes separate.

④ New cells form during cytokinesis.

Mark It Up

Highlight the part of the drawing that shows how each cell gets only one set of genetic material.

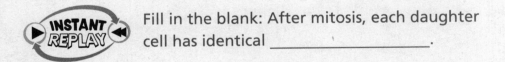

INSTANT REPLAY   Fill in the blank: After mitosis, each daughter cell has identical _____.

Cytokinesis

During cytokinesis the parent cell's cytoplasm divides. Cytokinesis happens after mitosis. The cell pinches together at the middle. This separates the parent cell's cytoplasm into two. At the end of cytokinesis, the two new cells are completely separated. Each cell is surrounded by a cell membrane. Each cell has a full set of DNA.

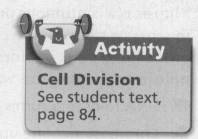

Activity

Cell Division
See student text, page 84.

The new cells continue the cell cycle. They are now back in interphase, growing and carrying out regular functions.

After cytokinesis, how many cells are there?

_____

SECTION 3.2	
SUMMARIZE	**VOCABULARY**
1. Imagine that a cell goes through mitosis and cytokinesis. Draw the cells that result.	Draw a line to connect each word to its definition. 2. cell cycle a. when a cell grows and carries out normal functions 3. interphase b. division of the cytoplasm 4. mitosis c. division of the nucleus 5. cytokinesis d. life cycle of a cell

SECTION

3.3

Key Concept
Both sexual and asexual reproduction involve cell division.

Student text pages 88–92

What is asexual reproduction?

Some living things produce offspring that are genetically the same as the parent. In **asexual reproduction** one parent produces offspring that have the same exact DNA. Asexual means *not* sexual. Some types of asexual reproduction are described below.

 How many parent organisms are involved in asexual reproduction?

_____

Mitosis

A single-celled organism reproduces each time it divides. This is a type of asexual reproduction because the offspring have the same DNA as the parent. Both single-celled eukaryotes and prokaryotes may reproduce through cell division. A eukaryotic cell—a cell with a nucleus—divides by mitosis and cytokinesis.

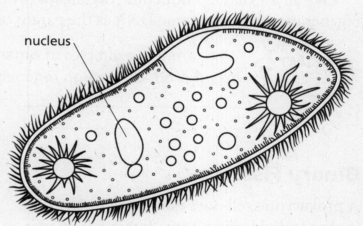

nucleus

Single-celled eukaryotes, like this one, may reproduce through mitosis and cytokinesis.

 Fill in the blanks: Single-celled eukaryotes may reproduce through _____ and

_____.

Regeneration

Some multicellular organisms can reproduce by regeneration. **Regeneration** is a process in which a body part gets broken off and grows into a whole new organism.

 What is one way that some multicellular organisms can reproduce?

_____

If one arm of this sea star breaks off, it may grow into a whole new organism.

The sea star is one animal that can reproduce through regeneration. If one of the sea star's arms gets broken off, it may grow into a new individual. Many plants can also reproduce this way. If a stem of a plant is cut off, the cut may heal, and the plant will keep growing. But the part that was cut off may also grow into a whole new plant.

Like all asexual reproduction, organisms produced by regeneration have the same DNA as the parent organism.

 What are two examples of organisms that may reproduce through regeneration?

_____

_____

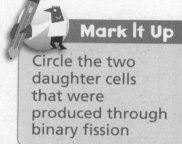 **Mark It Up**

Circle the two daughter cells that were produced through binary fission

Binary Fission

A prokaryotic cell does not have a nucleus, so it cannot divide by mitosis. Instead, it divides through a process called binary fission.

In **binary fission** the parent cell's DNA is replicated, or copied, and then the cell splits in two. This is different than mitosis because the cell does not have a nucleus that is divided.

 Fill in the blank: Single-celled prokaryotes may reproduce through _____.

Binary Fission

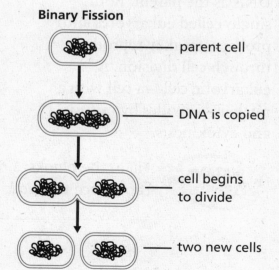

parent cell

DNA is copied

cell begins to divide

two new cells

Prokaryotes do not have a nucleus, so they reproduce through binary fission.

What is sexual reproduction?

Sexual reproduction is different from asexual reproduction. In sexual reproduction, the offspring get their DNA from two parents. The offspring are not exactly the same as either parent. The chart below compares asexual reproduction with sexual reproduction.

	Asexual Reproduction	Sexual Reproduction
Number of Parents	one	two
Offspring's Genes	identical to parent's	not identical to parents'

How many parent organisms are involved in sexual reproduction?

_____

SECTION 3.3

SUMMARIZE	VOCABULARY
1. What are two ways in which asexual reproduction is different from sexual reproduction? _____ _____ _____ _____ _____	Circle the word that makes each sentence correct. 2. Binary fission is one example of **asexual / sexual** reproduction. 3. Cells that do not have a nucleus divide through **regeneration / binary fission.**

Review CHAPTER

3 Cell Division

CLASSZONE.COM

Go to ClassZone.com for activities, links, and more test practice.

Vocabulary

Choose a word from the box, and write it next to its definition.

1 A chromosome is made of packaged _____.

2 Two main parts of cell division are _____ and _____.

3 In unicellular organisms, cell division is a form of _____.

asexual reproduction
chromosome
cytokinesis
DNA
mitosis

Reviewing Key Concepts

4 What is the name of the structure in the picture? _____

5 Look at the picture. This structure contains two identical copies of DNA. Draw a circle around each of the identical parts of this structure.

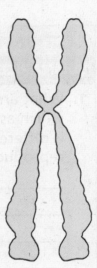

the BIG idea

6 List the functions of cell division for unicellular and multicellular organisms.
Unicellular organisms: _____
Multicellular organisms: _____

Test Practice

7 Which process of cell division results in two identical cells?

A mitosis

B osmosis

C diffusion

D interphase

8 Where is a chromosome found?

A in the lysosome

B in the membrane

C in the nucleus

D in the Gogli apparatus

CHAPTER
4 Patterns of Heredity

the BIG idea

In sexual reproduction, genes are passed from parents to offspring in predictable patterns.

Getting Ready to Learn

Review Concepts

- Cells come from other cells.
- Mitosis produces cells that are genetically identical.
- Some organisms reproduce through asexual reproduction.

Activity

Mendel's Experiment
See student text, page 99.

Review Vocabulary

Match each word with its definition.

_____ **DNA**

_____ **chromosome**

_____ **mitosis**

_____ **asexual reproduction**

a. produces genetically identical offspring

b. molecule that makes up the genetic information

c. part of cell division that divides the nucleus

d. tightly packaged DNA

Preview Key Vocabulary

As you read the chapter, write a sentence describing how each pair of words is related.

gene and allele

_____

_____

meiosis and gamete

_____

_____

SECTION
4.1

Key Concept
Living things inherit traits in patterns.

Student text pages
101–107

What is sexual reproduction?

Asexual reproduction involves one parent. In asexual reproduction the offspring have the same DNA as the parent.

Offspring produced by sexual reproduction have two parents. These offspring are not identical to their parents. During **sexual reproduction** each parent contributes one cell with genetic information. The two cells combine and form the offspring.

 In sexual reproduction, how many parents are involved?

_____

The offspring of sexual reproduction are not identical to either of the parents. But the offspring have similar characteristics, or traits. Your hair color, eye color, and blood type may be the same as your parents'. These are inherited traits. Inherited traits are characteristics you got from your parents. These traits are coded in the DNA your parents gave you.

Not all your traits came from your parents' DNA. Some traits are things that you acquired* during your life. Things you learned are acquired traits. Your ability to read and write are acquired traits.

This student's hair color is an inherited trait. But his ability to play the violin was acquired.

 Which traits may be passed on to offspring through genetic information—acquired traits or inherited traits?

_____

*Academic Vocabulary: **Acquire** means you get or gain something. When you put a coin in a gumball machine, you **acquire** a piece of candy.

What is a gene?

DNA is a molecule that makes up all of your genetic information. DNA that is tightly wound up forms a chromosome. Your chromosomes each contain hundreds of genes. A **gene** is a segment* of DNA that leads to a particular trait. Most traits are not determined by just one gene. Instead, most traits are affected by the interaction of many genes.

The offspring of sexual reproduction have similar traits as both parents. This is because offspring get half their chromosomes—and therefore, half their genes—from each parent.

 What is a gene? Underline the sentence above that tells you.

Visual Connection
See Human Chromosomes in the student text, page 103.

Chromosome Pairs

Before sexual reproduction happens, chromosomes are copied. Copied chromosomes have two identical parts that are attached in the middle. A copied chromosome looks like the letter *X*.

Before the chromosome is copied it looks like the letter *l*. You can see this in the picture.

 How is the chromosome in the drawing on the left different from the chromosome on the right?

_____

Chromosomes come in pairs. Each human body cell has 46 chromosomes. These 46 chromosomes are really two complete sets of DNA, so there are 23 chromosome pairs. You inherited one set of 23 chromosomes from your mother and one set from your father.

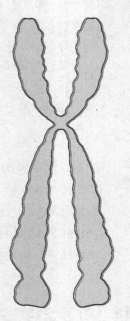

This copied chromosome has two identical parts.

Each copy looks like this.

*Academic Vocabulary: **Segment** means a piece of something larger. One centimeter is a **segment** on a meterstick.

Genes and Alleles

Each of the two chromosomes in a pair contain the same genes. But they might have different forms of the genes. Different forms of the same gene are called **alleles** (uh-LEELZ). In the picture, you can see a gene for plant height. Both chromosomes have a gene for plant height. The gene is on the same place on each chromosome. But each chromosome has a different form of the gene. One chromosome has the regular height allele (*H*) and the other has the short height allele (*h*).

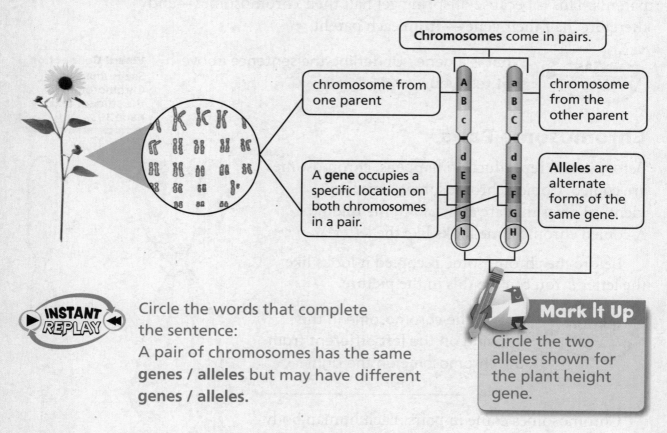

Chromosomes come in pairs.

chromosome from one parent

chromosome from the other parent

A **gene** occupies a specific location on both chromosomes in a pair.

Alleles are alternate forms of the same gene.

▶ **INSTANT REPLAY** ◀

Circle the words that complete the sentence:
A pair of chromosomes has the same **genes / alleles** but may have different **genes / alleles**.

Mark It Up

Circle the two alleles shown for the plant height gene.

Who was Gregor Mendel?

Gregor Mendel studied heredity. **Heredity** is the passing of genes from parents to offspring. Mendel studied pea plants. He chose two different pea plants as parents and bred them. Then, he compared the parents' and the offsprings' traits. He tested many different traits with many different pea plants.

Mendel noticed patterns in the way traits were inherited. Today, scientists understand that different alleles produce the patterns that Mendel saw.

 What did Mendel use pea plants to study?

_____

How do alleles interact to produce traits?

Most traits are not controlled by only one gene. Most traits are caused by many different genes. But it is helpful to look at traits caused by only one gene to learn about heredity.

A trait that is controlled by a single gene still involves two alleles. Remember that each chromosome of a pair will have one allele. The interaction of these two alleles determines the trait.

 If a trait is controlled by a single gene, how many alleles are involved? _____

Phenotype and Genotype

When you think about heredity, you might think about the genetic information that causes that trait. All of the traits you can see are part of a phenotype. Your eye color and your height are parts of your **phenotype.** All of the alleles the organism has is a **genotype.** You cannot see an organism's genotype.

 Circle the correct word to complete the sentence: Hair color is part of an organism's **phenotype / genotype.**

Dominant and Recessive Alleles

You just read that phenotype (traits) is caused by genotype (alleles). But if a living thing has two different alleles, what trait will it get?

The trait that a living thing gets depends on how the alleles interact. Some alleles are dominant. A **dominant** allele is one that appears, or is expressed, even if there is only one copy of the allele in the genotype. A **recessive** allele is only expressed if there are two copies of it—one on each chromosome of a pair.

Look at the picture. This plant has two different alleles for height: an allele for regular height (*H*) and an allele for short height (*h*). The plant's genotype is *Hh*. You can see the plant's alleles on the chromosomes. There is one of each allele in the genotype. So what will the plant's phenotype be?

The traits expressed in the phenotype depend on how the two alleles interact. The allele for regular height is dominant. Even though there is only one allele for regular height, the plant will be of regular height. Only plants with two alleles for short height, the recessive allele, will have a short phenotype.

Mark It Up

Circle the part of this drawing that is the phenotype. Highlight the part that is the genotype.

  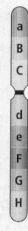

This tall plant has one recessive allele and one dominant allele (*Hh*).

Which allele will be expressed even if there is only one copy of that allele?

_____

SECTION 4.1	
SUMMARIZE	**VOCABULARY**
1. Why do the offspring of sexual reproduction have traits that are similar to both parents? _____ _____ _____ _____ _____	Fill in each blank with the correct word. **genes** **alleles** 2. A pair of chromosomes contains the same _____. 3. A pair of chromosomes may have different _____.

Student text pages 110–115

What is a Punnett square?

A tool that can be used to predict traits of offspring is called a Punnett square. A **Punnett square** shows how two parents' alleles might combine in offspring.

A Punnett square is shown here. It predicts patterns of the height of the offspring of two parent plants. One parent plant has two regular height alleles (*HH*). The other parent has two short height alleles (*hh*).

The two alleles of one parent are written across the top of the square. The two alleles of the other parent are written along the side of the square. The four boxes show all the possible ways that the parents' alleles can combine.

Activity

Probability
See student text, page 110.

CLASSZONE.COM

Simulation Predict offspring traits with virtual Punnett squares.

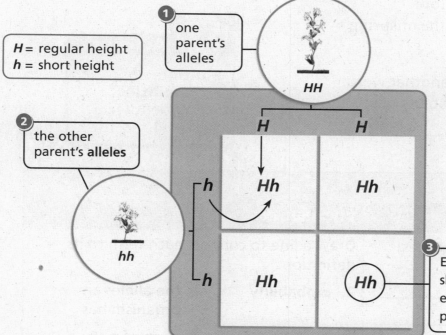

H = regular height
h = short height

① one parent's alleles

HH

② the other parent's alleles

hh

	H	*H*
h	*Hh*	*Hh*
h	*Hh*	*Hh*

Mark It Up

Highlight all of the alleles that come from one parent. Use a pencil to circle the alleles that came from the other.

③ Each box in the Punnett square shows one way the **alleles** from each parent could combine in potential offspring.

INSTANT REPLAY

Look at the Punnett square, and circle the word that completes the sentence: All the offspring of these two parents will be of **regular / short** height.

How are predictions of heredity expressed?

Punnett squares do not show actual offspring. Punnett squares only help to predict the probability that any one offspring will inherit a trait. A **probability** is the likelihood, or chance, that something will happen. Probability is given as a fraction or percent. In the earlier example, four out of four of the offspring (100 percent) will be *Hh*.

Now look at the Punnet square on this page. Two of the boxes have *Hh*. So two out of four (50 percent) of the offspring will be *Hh*. One of the boxes has *HH*, and another one has *hh*. There is a one out of four (25 percent) chance that the offspring will be either *HH* or *hh*.

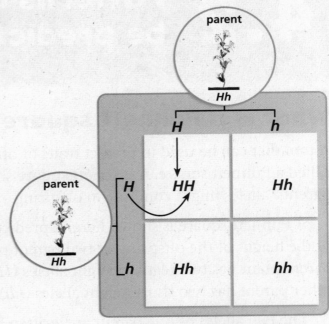

Punnet squares predict how likely an offspring will have a genotype.
1/4 will be HH.
2/4 will be Hh.
1/4 will be hh.

INSTANT REPLAY What is another word for probability?

_____

Activity

Multiple Probabilities
See student text, page 114.

SECTION 4.2

SUMMARIZE	VOCABULARY
1. What are Punnett squares used for? _____ _____ _____ _____ _____ _____	Draw a line to connect each term to its definition.

2. probability   **a.** the alleles an organism has

3. Punnett square   **b.** form of a gene

4. genotype   **c.** tool to predict patterns of heredity

5. allele   **d.** likelihood

SECTION 4.3

Key Concept

DNA is divided during meiosis.

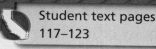

Student text pages 117–123

What is meiosis?

During sexual reproduction, DNA from two cells combines. But before the cells can combine, they need to have fewer chromosomes. Why? Human cells have 46 chromosomes. If two of these cells combined, the new cell would have 46 + 46 = 92 chromosomes. That is too many!

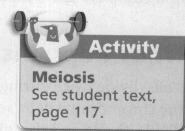

Activity

Meiosis
See student text, page 117.

The offspring of sexual reproduction do not inherit all of the chromosomes from each parent. Instead, they inherit half of their chromosomes from each parent. **Meiosis** is a process that produces cells with half the usual number of chromosomes. In humans, meiosis produces cells with 23 chromosomes.

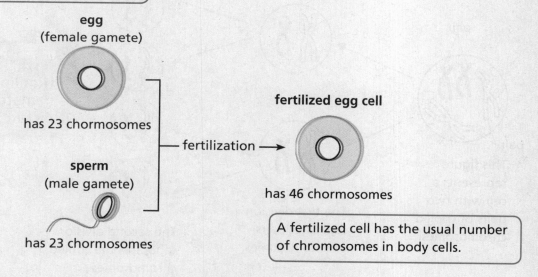

The egg and sperm each have half the usual number of chromosomes.

egg
(female gamete)

has 23 chormosomes

sperm
(male gamete)

has 23 chormosomes

fertilization →

fertilized egg cell

has 46 chormosomes

A fertilized cell has the usual number of chromosomes in body cells.

What is meiosis?

_____

Cells that are produced by meiosis are called gametes. **Gametes** have half the usual number of chromosomes—one chromosome from each pair. An **egg** is a gamete that forms in the female reproductive organs.

A **sperm** is a gamete that forms in the male reproductive organs. In humans, each gamete has 23 chromosomes. When they combine (23 + 23 = 46 chromosomes), they form a cell with the usual number for human body cells. The combination of an egg and sperm to form a new complete cell is called **fertilization.**

What happens during meiosis?

Cells divide twice during meiosis. The first time the cells divide, the chromosome pairs separate. The second time the cells divide, the copied chromosomes separate.

Visual Connection
See Meiosis in the student text, page 121.

Look at the picture. A cell starts with a full set of copied pairs of chromosomes. Each chromosome looks like an *X*. The two similar *X*'s are one chromosome pair. The first division separates the pairs of chromosomes. The result is two cells with only one of the chromosomes from each pair.

Meiosis results in gametes with half the usual number of chromosomes.

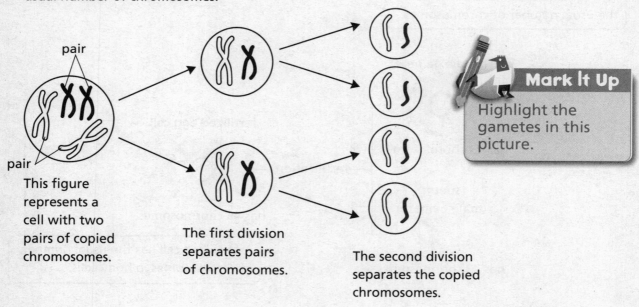

pair

pair

This figure represents a cell with two pairs of copied chromosomes.

The first division separates pairs of chromosomes.

The second division separates the copied chromosomes.

Mark It Up

Highlight the gametes in this picture.

What gets separated in the first division of meiosis?

_____

The second division separates each copied chromosome. The result is four gametes. A gamete is a cell with half the number of chromosomes as a body cell. In the drawing, each gamete has two chromosomes.

 What gets separated in the second division of meiosis?

_____

How do meiosis and mitosis differ?

Meiosis and mitosis are both types of cell division. But they are different. Here are some of the important differences.

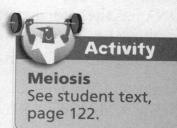

Activity

Meiosis
See student text, page 122.

- **Types of cells** Only cells in the reproductive organs will go through meiosis. All other cells divide by mitosis.

- **Number of times the cell divides** During meiosis, a cell divides twice. During mitosis, a cell divides only once.

- **Number of chromosomes in the final cells** Meiosis produces cells with half as many chromosomes as the parent cell. Mitosis produces cells with the same number of chromosomes as the parent cell.

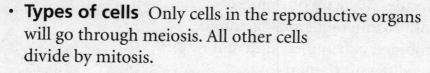 List at least two differences between meiosis and mitosis.

_____

_____

SECTION 4.3	
SUMMARIZE	**VOCABULARY**
1. What is produced by the process of meiosis? _____ _____ _____ _____ _____	Fill in each blank with the correct word. **gamete** **fertilization** **meiosis** 2. The joining of an egg and sperm is called _____. 3. Gametes are produced through _____. 4. A type of cell that results from meiosis is called a _____.

Student text pages
125–133

What is the information in DNA used for?

DNA has the information that a cell uses to make proteins. Proteins do most of the work in a cell. They also make up important parts of a cell's structure.

Proteins are large molecules made up of chains of amino acids. There are only 20 different kinds of amino acids. But they can be combined in countless different ways. Each combination makes a different protein.

Activity

Templates
See student text, page 125.

What are two functions of proteins in cells?

_____ _____

What process makes copies of DNA?

Each cell has only one copy of DNA. But before a cell divides, it needs to copy its DNA. The process by which DNA is copied is called replication.

Visual Connection
See Replication in the student text, page 127.

What is replication?

_____

What is the function of RNA?

Before a protein is made, DNA must pass its information to an RNA molecule. RNA stands for ribonucleic acid. RNA is a molecule that uses the information in DNA to connect amino acids into proteins.

 CLASSZONE.COM

Visualization Watch an animation of how proteins are made.

There are two main steps to make proteins.

① The information in the DNA molecule is transferred into an RNA molecule. This process is called transcription.

② The information in the RNA molecule is used to connect certain amino acids together to form the different proteins the cell needs. This process is called translation.

Activity

Transcription
See student text, page 131.

Making Proteins

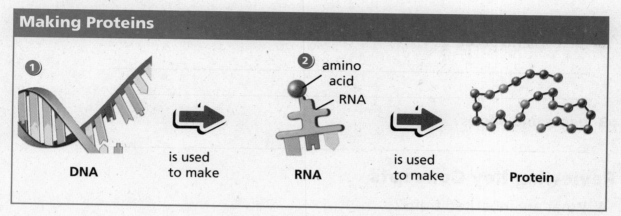

① DNA — is used to make — ② amino acid / RNA — RNA — is used to make — Protein

The information in DNA is transferred to RNA. What is the information in the RNA molecule then used for?

_____

SECTION 4.4	
SUMMARIZE	**VOCABULARY**
1. At the end of transcription and translation, what type of molecule is made from the information stored in DNA? _____ _____	Fill in each blank with the correct word from the list. DNA protein RNA The information in **2.** _____ is transferred to **3.** _____, which then puts together amino acids to form **4.** _____.

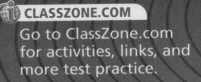

CLASSZONE.COM
Go to ClassZone.com for activities, links, and more test practice.

Vocabulary

Explain the relationship between each pair of words.

1 sexual reproduction and meiosis

_____

2 meiosis and gametes

_____

_____

3 genes and alleles

_____

Reviewing Key Concepts

4 What are inherited traits?

_____

5 How are gametes—the cells produced by meiosis—different from regular body cells?

_____

the BIG idea

6 In sexual reproduction, how much of each parent's genes are passed to offspring?

_____

Test Practice

7 Which process of cell division produces gametes for sexual reproduction?

A mitosis
B osmosis
C diffusion
D meiosis

8 A gene is a segment of

A RNA
B DNA
C protein
D alleles

5 Views of Earth's Past

the **BIG** idea

Rocks, fossils, and other types of natural evidence tell Earth's story.

Getting Ready to Learn

Review Concepts

- Unicellular organisms have only one cell, but multicellular organisms have many cells and specialized parts.
- Earth's surface is made up of large plates that interact.

Activity

Earth's History
See student text, page 149.

Review Vocabulary

Write the correct term for each description.

fossil   **igneous rock**   **metamorphic rock**   **sedimentary rock**

Rock changed by heat or pressure _____

Rock that started as hot liquid _____

A trace or remains of an organism from long ago _____

Rock that forms from pieces of older rocks _____

Preview Key Vocabulary

As you read, use the frames to write important details about each of the terms below.

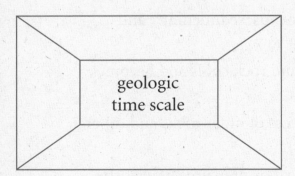

geologic time scale

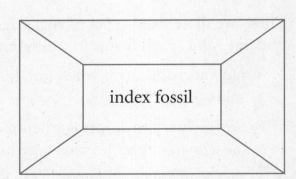

index fossil

SECTION
5.1

Key Concept
Rocks provide a timeline for Earth.

Student text pages
151–158

What is relative age?

Sometimes it is difficult to know exactly when something happened. But it can be easy tell the order that events happened. For example, you might know that a friend has an older brother and a younger brother without knowing the exact ages of her brothers.

If you know the order of when events happened, you know their relative ages. **Relative age** is the age of an event or object compared to other events or objects. Geologists use the relative ages of rocks and fossils to learn about Earth's history.

INSTANT REPLAY What are the relative ages of the events below? Number them in the order they happened.

_____ you were born

_____ you went to 6th grade

_____ your parents were born

_____ you went to 2nd grade

How do the three main types of rocks form?

There are three main types of rocks: igneous, sedimentary, and metamorphic. Each forms in a different way.

- Igneous rock forms when hot, liquid rock cools and becomes solid.

- Sedimentary rock forms when pieces of older rocks and other loose material get pressed together.

- Metamorphic rock forms when heat or pressure changes the structure of an existing rock.

INSTANT REPLAY Circle the names of the three main types of rocks.

Over thousands to millions of years, rocks change, break down, and re-form into other types of rocks. The **rock cycle** is a set of natural processes that changes each type of rock into other types. You can see how rocks change by the rock cycle in the drawing below.

Visual Connection
See Rock Cycle in the student text, page 153.

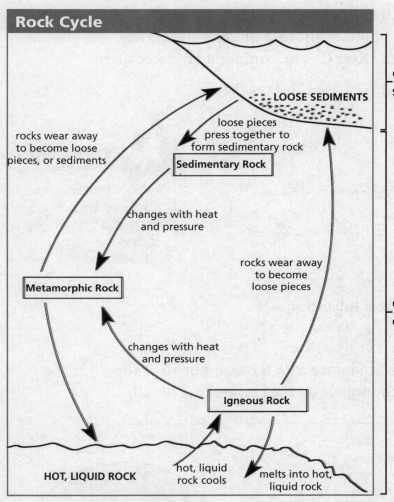

Rock Cycle

earth's surface

LOOSE SEDIMENTS

rocks wear away to become loose pieces, or sediments

loose pieces press together to form sedimentary rock

Sedimentary Rock

changes with heat and pressure

rocks wear away to become loose pieces

Metamorphic Rock

earth's crust

changes with heat and pressure

Igneous Rock

HOT, LIQUID ROCK

hot, liquid rock cools

melts into hot, liquid rock

Mark It Up

Circle the verbs next to each arrow. They will tell you how rocks change.

Over thousands to millions of years, rocks change through the processes of the rock cycle.

What is the rock cycle?

_____

_____

How do rock layers show relative age?

You can see in the photo that sedimentary rock looks striped. This is because it formed in layers. Each layer forms when loose pieces of rock and other things piles on top of a layer that is already formed.

Sedimentary Rock

Sedimentary rock looks striped because it was formed one layer at a time.

Over time, different layers of sedimentary rock will build up. Each layer of rock contains clues about life on Earth when the rock layer formed. New layers of rock form on top of older layers. So the oldest layer within a sedimentary rock is on the very bottom. The newest, or youngest, layer is on the top.

Geologists can use the order of layers to tell the relative ages of different rock layers. Look at the photo. It shows a piece of rock. The bottom layer, A, is the oldest layer. Layer C is the youngest layer because it is on top.

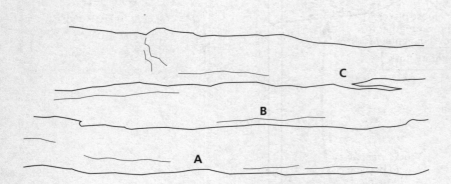

C

B

A

Mark It Up

Label the oldest, middle, and youngest layers of rock.

A particular rock layer is as old as the fossils within that layer.

Which layer of sedimentary rock is older, one near the bottom or near the top of a set of layers?

_____

Index Fossils

Sometimes pieces of living things, such as leaves or bones, might fall on top of a rock. If a new layer forms on top of it, the living thing might become a fossil. A fossil is a trace* or the remains of a once-living thing from long ago.

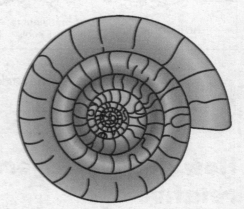

This fusulinid is a fossil of an ancient animal that is no longer found on Earth.

*Academic Vocabulary: **Trace** means evidence of an organism or thing that was once alive or present. Crumbs on a plate may be the leftover **trace** of a slice of cake.

Fossils can give clues about the age of the rock. Fossilized organisms in a rock layer likely lived during the same time when that particular rock layer formed. Look at the drawing. It shows a piece of sedimentary rock with fossils in it. The fossils in the bottom layers are older than the fossils in the top layers.

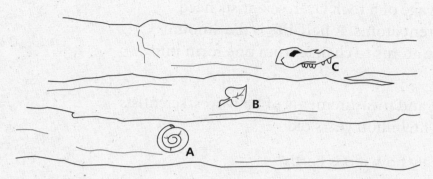

Fossil A is the oldest because it is in the bottom layer of rock.
Fossil C is the youngest because it is in the top layer of rock.

Scientists have determined the ages of many different types of fossilized organisms. Fossils of organisms that were common, that lived in many areas, and that lived only during specific time spans are called **index fossils.** These characteristics of index fossils make them especially useful for figuring out the ages of rock layers.

 What is an index fossil? Underline the sentence that tells you.

How is the actual age of rocks determined?

In addition to knowing someone's relative age—if the person is older or younger—you might also know the person's actual age, or age in years. The actual, or exact, age of rocks can also be determined. The actual age of an event or object is called **absolute age.**

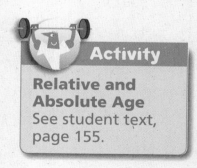

Activity

Relative and Absolute Age
See student text, page 155.

 What is your absolute age?

_____

Half-Life

Scientists can use radiometric dating to learn the absolute age of a fossil. In radiometric dating, scientists measure the amount of certain atoms in rock layers. Then they can use math to find out the age of the layers.

Visual Connection
See Radioactive Breakdown and Dating Rock Layers in the student text, page 157.

Before they can know the age of a rock layer, scientists need to know the half-life of different atoms. A **half-life** is the amount of time it takes for half of the atoms to change from one form into another form.

Using radiometric dating and measurements of half-lives, scientists estimate that Earth is about 4.6 billion years old.

 Approximately how old is Earth?

_____

SECTION 5.1	
SUMMARIZE	**VOCABULARY**
1. What are three types of information from rocks that can be used to tell the story of Earth's past? 1. _____ 2. _____ 3. _____ _____	Circle the word that makes each sentence correct. **2.** Rocks change from one type into another through the processes of the **index fossil / rock cycle.** **3.** A comparison of sedimentary rock layers gives information about **relative age / absolute age.** **4.** The **relative age / absolute age** of Earth is 4.6 billion years.

Student text pages
160–167

How does Earth change?

Earth is constantly changing. There are many different processes that change Earth. Some of these are slow. Some of these are fast.

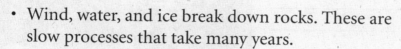

Activity

Time Scales
See student text, page 160.

- Wind, water, and ice break down rocks. These are slow processes that take many years.

- Volcanic eruptions can make new rocks. This can be a fast process that can take only days.

These processes change Earth today, and they are the same processes that changed Earth in the past. This is called the theory of **uniformitarianism** (YOO-nuh-fawr-mih-TAIR-ee-uh-nihz-uhm).

 Highlight a process that can quickly form new rocks.

How quickly do changes happen?

Some changes on Earth happen fast. An earthquake or the eruption of a volcano can cause huge changes in minutes or days. The photo below shows what Mount St. Helens looked like after an eruption.

When Mount St. Helens erupted, the eruption broke the top of the volcano.

Other changes are slow. Rain and wind wear down mountains. But it takes a long time. The river that wore away the rocks in the photo probably did this over millions of years.

river

Give one example of a slow process that changes Earth, making large changes over time. _____
_____
_____

What is the geologic time scale?

Earth is 4.6 billion years old. Scientists have organized those 4.6 billion years of Earth's history into a chart. The chart of Earth's history is called the **geologic time scale.** The geologic time scale divides Earth's history into sections. Major events or changes on Earth, including asteroid impacts or volcanic eruptions, mark the end of one section of the geologic time scale and the beginning of the next.

Visual Connection
See Geologic Time Scale in the student text, page 164.

What is the geological time scale?
_____
_____

SECTION 5.2	
SUMMARIZE	**VOCABULARY**
1. What causes the end or the beginning of each section in geologic time? _____ _____ _____ _____ _____	Write a brief definition for each term. 2. uniformitarianism _____ _____ 3. geologic time scale _____ _____

Student text pages 170–176

What do fossils and original remains tell about the past?

Fossils are traces or remains of living things from long ago. They provide important clues about past events. You read that index fossils help scientists determine the ages of rock layers. Fossils can also tell us about organisms that are now extinct. Organism's that are extinct, such as dinosaurs, once were living, but no longer exist.

Activity

Rocks
See student text, page 170.

Fossils in Rocks

There are many different types of fossils. Some fossils are hard pieces of animals, such as shells, bones, or teeth. Other fossils form when minerals replace the remains* of an organism that is buried in the loose pieces that make up a layer of rock. Some fossils show evidence of an animal's movement, such as footprints.

Visual Connection
See Fossils in Rocks in the student text, page 173.

These fossil trilobites formed when minerals replaced the remains of the animals after they died.

What is one type of fossil?

_____

_____

*Academic Vocabulary: **Remains** are what is left over, such as the trunk of a dead tree.

Original Remains

Sometimes an actual organism may be preserved. Fossils that are the actual bodies or body parts of an organism are called **original remains.**

Mammoths are ancient animals that looked like elephants. Some of these animals were trapped in ice. The ice preserved* the mammoths. This means that when scientists find them, they look the same as they did when they were alive. Other animals are preserved when they are trapped by tar or a sticky material called amber. The photo shows the original remains of wasps that were trapped in amber.

Here are the original remains of wasps that were trapped and preserved in amber.

How are original remains different from rock fossils?

_____

_____

What can be learned from fossils, ice cores, and tree rings about changes in life and the environment ?

Fossils show that Earth has gone through many changes over billions of years. Fossils show the many different types of organisms that have lived on Earth. The fossil record also shows changes in the environment.

*Academic Vocabulary: **Preserved** means something has not aged or decayed. **Preservatives** in your food stop the food from going bad or growing bacteria that cause decay.

Other types of natural evidence can give information about more recent parts of Earth's past. In some areas of the world, thousands of years of snowfall have built up many layers of ice. Scientists can drill into the ice to take out **ice cores,** or long samples of the ice. Scientists can analyze the different layers of an ice core to learn about how the air has changed. The rings in tree trunks also give clues about environmental conditions.

 What are three types of natural evidence that can give information about changes in life and the environment?

_____ _____ _____

SECTION 5.3	
SUMMARIZE	**VOCABULARY**
1. Do fossils show that life and environmental conditions on Earth have changed or that they have mostly stayed the same? Explain your response. _____ _____ _____ _____ _____ _____	Write each term next to its description. **original remains ice core** **rock fossil** 2. Often shows hard parts of animals, such as shell or bone _____ 3. Can show changes in atmosphere conditions _____ 4. A frozen mammoth is one example _____

5 Views of Earth's Past

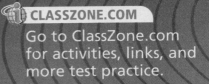
CLASSZONE.COM
Go to ClassZone.com
for activities, links, and
more test practice.

Vocabulary

Circle the word that completes each sentence.

1 Earth's history is organized in a chart called the
   geologic time scale / uniformitarianism.

2 **Fossils / half-lives** show traces of life from Earth's past.

3 The actual age of an object is its **relative age / absolute age.**

4 The order of the layers of sedimentary rock can show
   relative age / absolute age.

Reviewing Key Concepts

5 The processes of change on Earth today are similar to the
   processes of change in Earth's past. List at least three examples
   of processes that change Earth.

   _____

   _____

6 What is the rock cycle?

   _____

the BIG idea

7 List at least three types of evidence that scientists may study to
   learn about Earth's past.

   _____, _____, _____

Test Practice

8 How old is Earth?

   A 4.6 hundred years

   B 4.6 thousand years

   C 4.6 million years

   D 4.6 billion years

9 Fossils provide clues about

   A ice cores

   B Earth's past

   C the rock cycle

   D the half-life of igneous rocks

CHAPTER 6 Evolution of Living things

the **BIG** idea

Species develop and change over time.

Getting Ready to Learn

Review Concepts

- Earth formed over 4 billion years ago.
- Living things interact with their environment.
- Fossils are found in rock layers.

Activity

What Can Rocks Show About Earth's History? See student text, page 183.

Review Vocabulary

Draw a line to connect each word to its definition.

organism	an accepted scientific explanation
species	a group of living things of the same kind
theory	genetic material
DNA	an individual living thing

Preview Key Vocabulary

As you read the chapter, write words describing each term on the spokes of the description wheel diagrams.

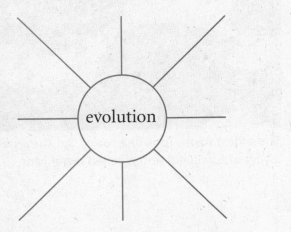

evolution

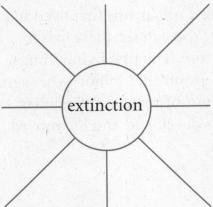

extinction

SECTION 6.1

Key Concept

Earth has been home to living things for about 3.8 billion years.

Student text pages 185–190

What do fossils tell about earlier life on Earth?

Fossils are traces or remains of living things from long ago. Some fossils are found in rock layers. Different rock layers contain fossils of different organisms. Each rock layer contains fossils of organisms that lived when that rock layer formed.

Activity

Fossils
See student text, page 185.

Scientists use the information in rocks and fossils to learn about the changes in life over the history of Earth. The information provided by fossils and their positions in rock layers is called the fossil record.

What is the fossil record? Underline the sentence that tells you.

How were the earliest life forms different from later life forms?

The first living things on Earth were single-celled organisms that lived in the ocean. You can see these fossils in the picture. The first living things appeared around 3.8 billion years ago. Over billions of years, multicellular organisms developed and life moved onto land.

The oldest fossils look like rocks, but they are really layers of fossilized single-celled organisms.

Prokaryotes

Fossil evidence shows that the earliest life forms were prokaryotes. A prokaryote is a unicellular, or single-celled, organism without a nucleus. Many groups of prokaryotes lived in the ocean.

The early prokaryotes used the process of photosynthesis to make sugars. They gave off oxygen as a waste product. Over time, this process led to changes in the atmosphere. One important change is that oxygen levels increased.

 What evidence shows that the earliest forms of life were prokaryotes? _____

Eukaryotes

As prokaryotes added oxygen to the atmosphere, organisms that used oxygen developed. These organisms are called eukaryotes. By looking at fossils, scientists think that the first eukaryotes developed about 2 billion years ago.

A eukaryote has its genetic material in a nucleus. Eukaryotes also have other organelles, such as mitochondria. Mitochondria use oxygen for cellular respiration.

The first eukaryotes were single-celled. Over time, multicellular organisms developed. The first multicellular organisms were algae. Seaweeds are an example of algae. They appeared about 1.5 billion years ago. Multicellular animals appeared about 600 million years ago. The first multicellular animals were like jellyfish.

Mark It Up

Highlight the part of the timeline when life was found only in the ocean.

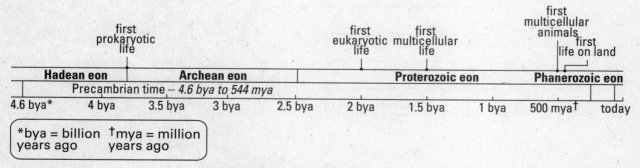

During much of Earth's history, only unicellular life existed.

Life on Land

All life stayed in the ocean for over 3 billion years. The fossil record shows that life moved to land about 460 million years ago. The first land organisms were bacteria and algae. The first animals on land were insects. Over time, these organisms spread to new areas and new life forms evolved. New life forms continued to evolve in the ocean, too.

Activity
Fossil Records
See student text, page 187.

Circle the phrase that completes the sentence:
For most of the history of life on Earth, life existed only **in the ocean / on land.**

What are mass extinctions?

Many different kinds of life forms have lived on Earth. But many have gone extinct. **Extinction** is the loss of all the members of a species. There have been several times in Earth's history when a lot of different species became extinct in a very short time. These events are called **mass extinctions.**

How is a mass extinction different from an extinction?

_____

_____

_____

_____

_____

_____

Most of these animals and plants died in a mass extinction. Once they were gone, dinosaurs became dominant.

A mass extinction may be caused by a major catastrophic* event. A catastrophic event is something that affects the whole Earth. For example, major volcanic eruptions may have caused one main mass extinction. Another main mass extinction was likely caused by an asteroid impact. The asteroid left a large crater off the coast of Mexico.

200 km

The impact left a 200-km-wide crater off the Yucatán peninsula in Mexico.

Some scientists think that something from space hit this part of Mexico a long time ago. It caused the large crater and probably caused a mass extinction.

What are two catastrophic events that may have caused mass extinctions?

_____   _____

*Academic Vocabulary: A **catastrophic** event is one that causes huge damage or changes the way things are. If a storm destroys a town, the town is experiencing a **catastrophe**.

SECTION 6.1	
SUMMARIZE	**VOCABULARY**
1. What are major catastrophic events? _____ _____ _____ _____ _____ _____	Fill in each blank with the correct term from the list. extinction mass extinction fossil record 2. The end of a species _____ 3. The information from fossils and their location in rocks _____ 4. The end of many species _____

Student text pages
191–199

How did the idea of biological evolution develop?

The word *evolution* can mean different things, depending on how the word is used. In general, evolution means change over time. Biological **evolution** is the process by which species change over time. Biological evolution is the result of changes in genetic material.

Underline the sentence that tells you what causes biological evolution.

A British naturalist named Charles Darwin spent decades* studying evolution in the mid-1800s. He used his many years of observations and studies to develop an explanation for the process by which evolution occurs. He called this process natural selection.

Visual Connection
See Darwin's Voyage in the student text, pages 192–193.

What is selection?

Selection means that certain traits occur more than others. There are two kinds of selection: artificial selection and natural selection.

In artificial selection, people control the traits in an organism. You are probably familiar with many different breeds of cats and dogs. A breeder mates two cats with certain desired traits. From their offspring, the breeder selects only the cats with the desired traits for the next round of mating. The process continues for many generations. Over time, a new breed can be produced.

Many different varieties of cats have been bred through artificial selection.

*Academic Vocabulary: A **decade** is ten years. On your tenth birthday, you were one **decade** old.

Darwin realized that a similar process happens in nature. This method is natural selection.

Natural selection is a process in which individuals with certain traits survive and reproduce more than individuals without those traits. In natural selection, the conditions in the environment determine whether one trait is chosen over another.

Visual Connection
See Natural Selection in the student text, page 197.

Look at the drawings. These show the beaks of some birds that Darwin observed. One type of bird had a large beak that could crush nuts. This bird survived best in areas where nuts were the main type of food. Another type of bird had a long, sharp beak that could cut into cactus. It survived best in areas where cacti were the main type of food.

This ground finch has a large beak. It can crush large nuts and eat them.

This cactus finch has a pointed beak. It can tear open a cactus and eat the plant's watery insides.

How is artificial selection different from natural selection? _____

_____

What are the parts of natural selection?

In natural selection, a population changes over time. A **population** is a group of organisms of the same species that live in the same area. There are four important parts of natural selection: overproduction, variation, adaptation, and selection.

Overproduction In nature, organisms have more offspring than their environment can support. This is called overproduction. Not all of the offspring will survive and reproduce.

Underline the sentence that tells you what overproduction is.

Variation Variations are different traits that are found in a species. For example, birds of the same species might have different-sized beaks. The beak of one bird might be slightly bigger than the beak of another. Many variations are a result of differences in DNA. Genetic differences within a population is called **genetic variation.** Genetic variation comes from the mixing of genes during sexual reproduction.

Fill in the blank: Variations are different _____ that are found in a species.

Adaptation An **adaptation** is an inherited trait that gives an organism an advantage in its environment. Look at the drawings. They show different kinds of birds' feet. Each foot shape allows the bird to have a certain lifestyle. The first foot shape is adapted to hold on to branches, so it is easier for this bird to live in trees. Another bird foot is adapted for swimming. This bird would survive best in or near water.

Selection Organisms with the best adaptations can survive better than other individuals.

Bird Foot Adaptations

Foot Shape	Advantage
	holding onto branches
	walking in shallow water
	catching animals to eat
	swimming in lakes and ponds

Different traits, such as birds' foot shapes, can have advantages in different environments.

These organisms can find or get food more easily. They can find mates better. They can hide better from their enemies. Organisms with the best adaptations will have more offspring. Over time, traits that give organisms the most advantages will become more and more common in the population. This is called selection.

Underline the sentence that tells you what selection is.

The four parts of natural selection work together. Populations produce more offspring than can survive. Those individuals with variations that help them live in their particular environment are more likely to survive and reproduce. They will pass these traits on to their offspring. Over time, the adaptation will become more common in the population.

How do new species develop?

Sometimes, a population of organisms may be split into two or more groups. Mountain ranges, changes in water levels, and many other factors can split apart a population. The separated populations may live in very different environments. This could cause the groups to have different adaptations.

Eventually, the two populations may be so different that they cannot breed with each other and have offspring. When populations are too different to breed with each other and produce offspring they are considered to be separate species. The evolution of a new species from an existing species is called **speciation.**

Visual Connection
See Speciation in the student text, page 198.

Under what conditions are two populations considered to be separate species?

_____

_____

SECTION 6.2	
SUMMARIZE	**VOCABULARY**
1. What is natural selection? _____ _____ _____ _____ _____	Fill in the blanks with the correct term. **genetic variation** **evolution** **speciation** 2. _____ is the evolution of a new species. 3. Natural selection is the process by which _____ happens. 4. Many differences within a population are due to _____.

Environmental changes can affect populations.

Student text pages 202–208

What stops a population from growing?

A population of living things needs certain things to survive. Living things need food, water, a place to live, and many other resources. If living things have plenty of resources, they will find it easier to survive. If living things need more resources, they will have a more difficult time surviving. Factors in the environment that limit population size are called **limiting factors.**

What keeps the size of a population from growing endlessly? _____

Population Growth

A population of living things grows in size if its environment has more resources than the population needs. A population can grow when it has more births than deaths. A population also grows due to immigration. **Immigration** is when individuals move into the environment and join the population.

What are two ways a population can increase in size?

_____

_____

_____

When wolves are removed from an area, deer populations grow. This is because the deer have more births, and fewer of them are eaten by wolves.

Population Decrease

If there are not enough resources, a population may decrease in size through deaths and emigration. **Emigration** is the movement of individuals out of a population.

Mark It Up

Circle the word that means the opposite of immigration.

Why can changes in the environment cause extinctions?

Environmental changes can cause extinctions. Environmental changes might affect limiting factors or make some adaptations less helpful.

When the environment changes, limiting factors can change too. Look at the photo. It shows an area that had all of its trees cut down. A change like this may destroy food that some organisms eat and provide fewer places for animals to live. It could also mean that there is more space for other organisms to live and grow. If the amount of resources changes, the size of some populations might change too.

When all the trees in an area are cut down, the amount of resources changes. There are fewer places for animals to hide and fewer things to eat.

Some environmental changes can cause extinctions. But these changes must be large enough that they affect the whole population. In the past, large catastrophic events have caused extinctions. Other times, the environment changed slowly over time. Some areas got warmer or colder. Some areas became more dry or wet. Changes in the environment affect natural selection by making certain traits more desirable than other traits.

Activity

Natural Selection
See student text,
page 206.

In natural selection, traits that help survival in a particular environment may become more common within a population. But if the environment changes, those adaptations may no longer help individuals to survive. As a result, a change in the environment may cause individuals to die off quickly. If all the members of a species die, the species becomes extinct.

Underline the sentence that tells you why a species might go extinct when the environment changes.

SECTION 6.3	
SUMMARIZE	**VOCABULARY**
1. How do environmental factors affect population sizes?	immigration emigration limiting factor population 2. Which term means an individual leaves its group? _____ 3. Which is the term for something in the environment that controls population sizes? _____ 4. Which term describes a group of individuals of the same species that live in the same place? _____ 5. A new individual joins a population. Which term does this describe? _____

Student text pages 210–216

What is a scientific theory?

In everyday life, people use the word theory to talk about a new idea or a feeling about something. In science, the word *theory* means something different. A scientific **theory** is an explanation about the natural world that is based on a wide range of scientific evidence. A theory is a scientific explanation that is widely accepted by scientists. The theory of natural selection is supported by many types of evidence, including fossil evidence, biological evidence, and genetic evidence.

Activity

Evidence
See student text, page 210.

INSTANT REPLAY

How is the scientific meaning of the word theory different from the everyday use of the word?

_____

_____

_____

_____

Mark It Up

Circle the names of three types of evidence that support the theory of natural selection.

How does fossil evidence support evolution?

The fossil record shows the history of life on Earth and the evolution of modern organisms. The fossil record contains fossils of organisms that are the ancestors of modern organisms. An **ancestor** is an early form of an organism from which later forms evolve.

INSTANT REPLAY

What is an ancestor? Underline the sentence that tells you.

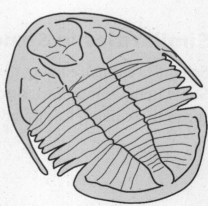

Fossils, such as this one, provide evidence to support the theory of natural selection.

By looking at fossils, scientists can compare how different living things looked throughout time. They found that some organisms from the past are very similar to ones that are alive today.

For example, some scientists use fossil evidence to hypothesize that birds evolved from dinosaurs. The drawing shows what an ancient bird might have looked like. The bird's fossils show that the bird had feathers. The fossils are also similar to dinosaur fossils. It has teeth and its skull and vertebrae look like those of dinosaurs. Although this evidence supports that birds we know today might have evolved from dinosaurs, there is not yet enough evidence to confirm it.

This illustration shows what an ancient bird might have looked like. The bird's fossil has feathers and looks like a bird, but its bones are similar to those of dinosaurs.

What biological evidence supports evolution?

Biological similarities among organisms give evidence that the organisms evolved from a common ancestor.

Visual Connection
See Biological Evidence for Evolution in the student text, page 213.

Similarities in Structure

Scientists compare living things by looking at their bodies. Some living things have similar organs and bones. This could mean these living things have a common* ancestor.

*Academic Vocabulary: **Common** means something that is shared. If you and your friends like the same music, you all have a **common** taste in music.

Vestigial Organs

Whales have tiny leg bones, but they do not have legs. Snakes also have tiny unused leg bones. Why do these animals have leg bones? Their leg bones are vestigial organs. **Vestigial organs** are structures that were fully developed in ancestral organisms but are small and unused in later species. Whales evolved from ancestors with legs. Similarly, the ancestors of snakes had legs. Living things with common bones might have a common ancestor.

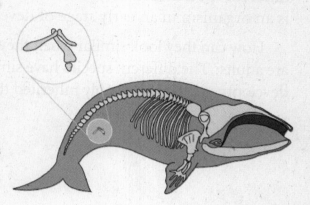

Leg bones are vestigial organs in whales. The leg bones are there, but they do not have a function.

Comparative Anatomy

The study of the similarities and differences of the physical structures of organisms is called comparative anatomy. Different species may have similar structures but use the structures in different ways.

For example, lizards, bats, and manatees all have similar bones in their forelimbs, or arms. One short bone goes from shoulder to elbow. Two long bones go from elbow to wrist. And five bones with joints come out from rounded wrist bones. The similar structures suggest that these organisms all shared a common ancestor.

The similar bone structures in their arms suggest that lizards, bats, and manatees share a common ancestor.

What does comparative anatomy give evidence for?

_____

_____

Similarities in Development

Your pet rabbit does not look like a chicken. But many animals from different species look very similar when they are embryos. An embryo is an organism in an early stage of development.

How can they look similar when they are embryos but not when they are adults? The different species have similar genes that control their early development. They probably inherited these genes from a common ancestor.

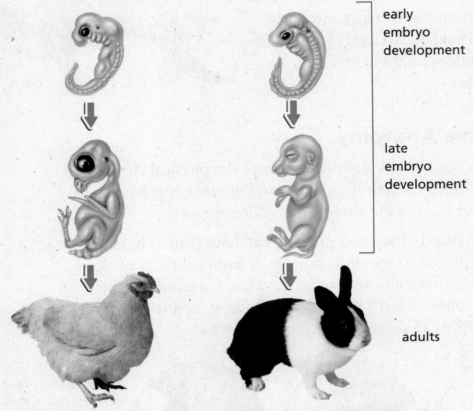

early embryo development

late embryo development

adults

The study of embryos shows that animals that look very different as adults are similar during early development.

Why do these organisms look similar as embryos?

_____

What genetic evidence supports evolution?

The study of DNA provides important information about evolution. DNA contains the information that organisms need to grow and develop. Genetic material is passed from parents to offspring.

DNA contains information that the cell uses to make the proteins it needs to live. The information is contained in the pattern of bases, which are the chemical pieces that make up DNA. There are four different DNA bases. The bases are represented with the letters A, T, C, and G.

Each gene is made up of a particular series of bases. Scientists can compare the sequences of bases that make up certain genes in different organisms. The more closely the bases match, the more closely related two species are. The genetic similarities in different organisms give evidence for common ancestors.

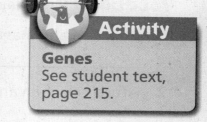

Activity

Genes
See student text, page 215.

What does it mean if two different species have strong similarities in their genes?

_____

SECTION 6.4	
SUMMARIZE	**VOCABULARY**
1. What are three types of evidence that scientists study to learn about evolution? _____ _____ _____	Fill in each blank with the correct term. **theory ancestor vestigial organ** 2. The whale's small and unused leg bones are an example of a _____. 3. A _____ is a widely accepted scientific explanation based on a wide range of evidence. 4. An _____ is an early form of an organism from which later forms evolved.

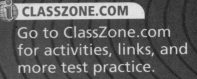

CLASSZONE.COM
Go to ClassZone.com for activities, links, and more test practice.

Vocabulary Explain the relationship between each pair of terms.

1 extinction and mass extinction

_____

2 natural selection and evolution

_____

3 adaptation and genetic variation

_____

Reviewing Key Concepts

4 What are two catastrophic events that can cause mass extinctions?

_____   _____

5 What is a scientific theory?

_____

6 What are three types of evidence that support evolution?

_____   _____   _____

the BIG idea

7 Describe the process of natural selection.

_____

_____

Test Practice

8 Which biological theory did Darwin develop using decades of observations and studies?

A meiosis
B mass extinction
C natural selection
D emigration

9 What accounts for much of the variation among individuals in a population?

A genetic variation
B the fossil record
C overproduction
D vestigial organs

7 Classification of Living Things

the **BIG** idea

Scientists have developed a system for classifying the great diversity of living things.

Getting Ready to Learn

Review Concepts

- Species change over time.
- Fossils and other evidence show that species change.
- The evolution of a new species from an existing species is called speciation.

Activity

How Would You Sort Pennies? See student text, page 227.

Review Vocabulary

Write the correct term for each description.

| evolution | ancestor | species | trait |

a relative that lived long ago   _____

a characteristic of an individual organism   _____

the changing of species over time   _____

a group of living things that can mate and produce offspring   _____

Preview Key Vocabulary

As you read, write the definition for each word below. Then sketch a picture in the space provided to help you remember the word's meaning.

Term	Definition	Sketch
cladogram		
vertebrate		
invertebrate		

Key Concept

Scientists develop systems for classifying living things.

 Student text pages 229–236

How do scientists identify different species?

You might have seen a guidebook that helps you identify* a bird or plant. Scientists also have ways to identify living things. They use a type of guide called a dichotomous key (dy-KAHT-uh-muhs).

CLASSZONE.COM

Simulation Use an interactive dichotomous key.

A dichotomous key is a tool that allows you to look at a living thing's traits and figure out what species it belongs to. You can see a dichotomous key here. The key describes a trait and asks you to find out whether your organism has that trait. Each choice you make leads to another description of a trait. Eventually, the observations and choices you make will allow you to identify the species.

INSTANT REPLAY

What is a dichotomous key used for?

_____

_____

_____

_____

_____

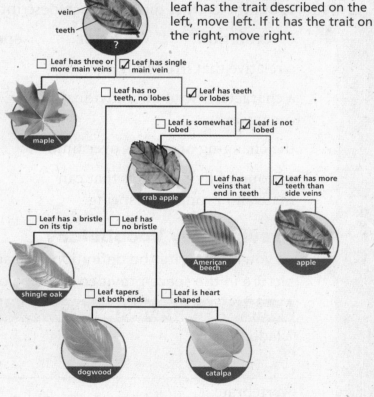

Start with the leaf at the top. Then look at the options below it. If your leaf has the trait described on the left, move left. If it has the trait on the right, move right.

☐ Leaf has three or more main veins
☑ Leaf has single main vein
☐ Leaf has no teeth, no lobes
☑ Leaf has teeth or lobes
☐ Leaf is somewhat lobed
☑ Leaf is not lobed
☐ Leaf has veins that end in teeth
☑ Leaf has more teeth than side veins
☐ Leaf has a bristle on its tip
☐ Leaf has no bristle
☐ Leaf tapers at both ends
☐ Leaf is heart shaped

maple · crab apple · American beech · apple · shingle oak · dogwood · catalpa

You can figure out what kind of leaf you are looking at by using a dichotomous key.

*Academic Vocabulary: **Identify** means to determine what something or who someone is. If you looked at a group of teachers at your school, you could **identify** which one is your science teacher.

How do scientists name species?

Scientists from different countries need to be able to communicate about different organisms. They need to be sure that when they use a name for a species, other scientists will know exactly which organism they are talking about. Today, scientists all use the same system for naming and classifying organisms into groups.

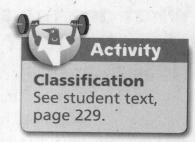

Activity

Classification
See student text, page 229.

Naming Species

The system that scientists use to name species is called binomial nomenclature (by-NOH-mee-uhl NOH-muhn-KLAY-chuhr). **Binomial nomenclature** is a system of naming things using two names for each type of organism.

Activity

Binomial Nomenclature
See student text, page 233.

The two parts of a species' name are called genus and species. A **genus** (JEE-nuhs) is a group of species that have similar characteristics. For example, many different types of bears belong to the genus *Ursus*. The second part of the name gives the particular species.

The picture below shows the scientific name of a house cat. Its scientific name, *Felis catus,* is written in italics.* The first letter of the genus is capitalized. The first letter of the species is lowercase.

Felis catus

This is the **genus** name.

This name describes the **species.**

Mark It Up

Circle the genus of a house cat.

INSTANT REPLAY What are the two parts of a name used in binomial nomenclature?

_____ _____

*Academic Vocabulary: Something written in **italics** is written in slanted letters. *This sentence is written in **italics.***

What are the seven levels of classification?

Classification is the process of sorting organisms into groups based on similarities. There are seven levels of the traditional system of classification. In order from largest to smallest, these are kingdom, phylum, class, order, family, genus, and species.

Visual Connection
See Classifying Organisms in the student text, page 235.

The highest level, kingdom, includes the largest number of species. Each level below that has fewer species. The smallest level, species, describes only one type of organism.

Each type of organism can be classified into a group at each level of organization. The more levels of organization a species shares with another species, the more closely related the two species are. For example, lions are more closely related to house cats than humans are. Humans are in the same class as house cats and lions. But lions and house cats are also in the same family.

 Which is the largest of the seven levels of organization? _____

SECTION 7.1	
SUMMARIZE	**VOCABULARY**

1. Put the seven levels of classification in order from largest to smallest: *order, genus, kingdom, class, phylum, species, family*
 	
_____
 	
_____
 	
_____
 	
_____
 	
_____
	Fill in each blank with the correct term from the list.
	
	   genus **classification**
	       binomial nomenclature
	
	Taxonomy is the science of naming and organizing organisms into groups.
	
	2. _____ is the system used for naming types of organisms. The first part of a scientific name is the
	
	3. _____ and the second part of the name is the species. The process of organizing organisms into groups is called
	
	4. _____ .

Branching diagrams show biological relationships.

Student text pages 238–245

How do scientists determine how organisms are related?

Living things that have a common ancestor are said to have an evolutionary relationship with each other. Scientists can determine if two species have a recent common ancestor by looking at physical and genetic evidence.

Physical evidence is gathered by observing traits, such as color, size, or different features. The picture shows an example of the kind of physical evidence scientists might use. Genetic evidence is gathered by comparing DNA among organisms.

Physical evidence, such as body shape, wings, feathers, and beaks, help you to tell that all of these animals are birds. It also tells you that these are different types of birds.

What two types of evidence do taxonomists use to classify organisms?

_____   _____

What do branching diagrams show?

A branching diagram is a line drawing that shows how closely related different living things are. Each line on a branching diagram shows one species. Each point on a branching diagram shows a time when two species developed from one. Each point represents a common ancestor.

 **INSTANT REPLAY** What is represented by a branch on the diagram that has split into two?

_____

Common Ancestors

If two species have a common ancestor, it means they evolved from the same species. You can find common ancestors on branching diagrams. Look at the diagram below. Each point shows when new species developed. The line before each point represents a common ancestor. The common ancestor of all four animals is shown at point B.

By looking at a branching diagram, you can tell which species are more closely related. Look at the red panda on the diagram. It shares a common ancestor with the raccoon more recently than it shares a common ancestor with the giant panda. This means the red panda is more closely related to the raccoon than to the giant panda.

Mark It Up

Circle the part of the diagram that shows the most recent common ancestor of the spectacled bear and the giant panda.

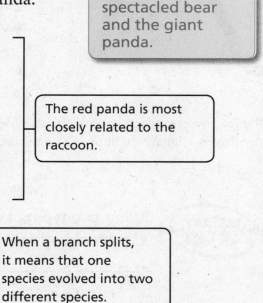

The red panda is most closely related to the raccoon.

When a branch splits, it means that one species evolved into two different species.

Cladograms

A **cladogram** (KLAD-uh-GRAM) is a branching diagram that shows how traits are passed from common ancestors. These traits give information about how the organisms evolved.

 **INSTANT REPLAY** What information are cladograms based on?

_____

The cladogram below shows the evolutionary history of plants. Like the branching diagrams you just looked at, the bottom line represents the common ancestor of all the species in the diagram.

Now find the cross-marks on the cladogram. Each is labeled with the name of a different trait. These marks show when a new trait developed. All of the organisms that branch off above that line have that trait. These kinds of traits are called derived characteristics. **Derived characteristics** are traits that have been changed from an earlier condition through evolution.

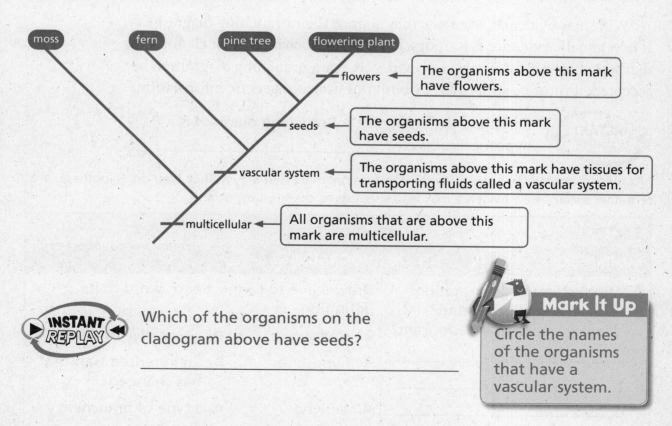

 **INSTANT REPLAY** Which of the organisms on the cladogram above have seeds?

_____

Mark It Up

Circle the names of the organisms that have a vascular system.

Cladograms do not show every trait that has evolved in organisms. Instead, they show traits that connect the evolutionary histories of species. When species appear lower on a cladogram, it does not mean that they have stopped evolving or that they are less evolved. It means that they shared an ancestor with the other species a very long time ago.

 What does it mean if an organism branches off lower on a cladogram? _____

_____

How are branching diagrams related to hypotheses?

The diagrams you have just seen show hypotheses about how organisms are related. A **hypothesis** is a tentative* explanation for an observation. Depending on the types of evidence used, different scientists may come up with different diagrams for the same organisms.

With new evidence, scientists may change their branching diagrams. If new genetic evidence is found, scientists might change older cladograms that were based only on physical evidence. For a branching diagram to be accepted, it must be supported by both physical and genetic information.

 Complete the sentence: A branching diagram is a hypothesis about _____.

*Academic Vocabulary: Something **tentative** is something that may change later on. Hypotheses are **tentative** because new evidence may lead scientists to change a hypothesis.

SECTION 7.2	
SUMMARIZE	**VOCABULARY**
1. What scientific information is shown on a branching diagram, such as a cladogram? _____ _____ _____ _____ _____	Draw a line to connect each word to its definition. 2. cladogram **a.** a tentative explanation 3. hypothesis **b.** an inherited trait that has changed 4. derived characteristic **c.** a type of branching diagram

Classification systems change as scientists learn more.

Student text pages 248–256

What are the groups we use to classify organisms?

In early classification systems, scientists put all organisms into two large groups: plants and animals. Today, most scientists use a system that divides organisms into three domains and six kingdoms.

Three domains

A domain is the highest level of classification. There are three domains. You can see these domains in the picture below.

One domain has only eukaryotes. Eukaryotes have cells with the genetic material enclosed in a nucleus.

The other two domains contain prokaryotes. Prokaryotes are single-celled organisms without a nucleus. Bacteria are in one domain, and archaea are in another domain. Although bacteria and archaea are both single-celled organisms with no nucleus, they are so genetically different that they are assigned to different domains.

What are the three domains?

_____ _____ _____

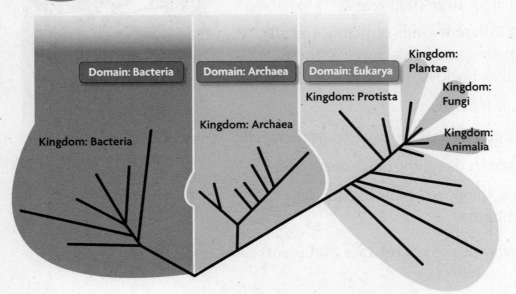

Here you can see how the three domains and the six kingdoms are related to each other.

Domain: Bacteria

Domain: Archaea

Domain: Eukarya

Kingdom: Plantae

Kingdom: Protista

Kingdom: Fungi

Kingdom: Animalia

Kingdom: Archaea

Kingdom: Bacteria

Six Kingdoms

Domains are divided into kingdoms. Today's classification system has six kingdoms: plants, animals, fungi, protists, bacteria, and archaea. Every known species on Earth is sorted into one of these six kingdoms.

Visual Connection
See Six Kingdoms in student text, page 250.

The number of groups of organisms has changed from the past, as scientists learn more about different species. Many scientists agree that three domains and six kingdoms is the best way to sort organisms based on the information we have today. However, some scientists think that the Kingdom Protista should be split into smaller kingdoms because of differences among its species. With new information, the organization might change again.

What are some of the characteristics of plants and animals?

The two most familiar kingdoms are Plantae and Animalia, the plants and animals.

Activity
Classifying Leaves
See student text, page 254.

Plants

Plants come in all shapes and sizes, from tiny mosses to giant sequoia trees. The oldest living organism on Earth is a plant called the bristlecone pine. Some bristlecone pines have been alive for over 4000 years!

There are many different kinds of plants, but all plants share certain characteristics. Some of these characteristics are listed below.

- Plants are multicellular.

- Plants store their DNA in the nucleus of their cells.

- Plants make sugars using the Sun's energy.

- Plant cells have tough cell walls outside of their cell membranes.

Trees have trunks and leaves. Mosses hang from trees and rocks. Although they look different, both are types of plants.

 Circle four characteristics that plants have.

Animals

Scientists have named a million species of animals. Whales, humans, bears, dogs, and other familiar organisms make up only a small percentage of all animal species. These organisms are **vertebrates,** or animals with backbones.

Monarch Butterfly

More than 90 percent of the known animal species are insects. Insects and many other types of organisms are **invertebrates,** or animals without backbones.

There are many different kinds of animals, but all animals share certain characteristics. Some of these characteristics are listed below.

Darkling Beetle

- Most animals have mouths and some type of nervous system.

- Animals store their DNA in the nucleus of their cells.

- Animals get their energy by eating other organisms.

- Animal cells do not have cell walls.

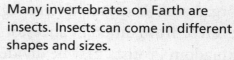

Many invertebrates on Earth are insects. Insects can come in different shapes and sizes.

 Circle the term that completes the sentence: Most animals are **vertebrates** / **invertebrates**.

What are some of the characteristics of the other kingdoms?

You might be able to think of examples of animals and plants. But the organisms in the other four kingdoms may be less familiar. You have probably seen—and maybe eaten—organisms from the kingdom Fungi. The other three kingdoms—Protista, Bacteria, and Archaea—consist mainly of organisms that are too small to see with just your eyes.

 Which three kingdoms consist mainly of organisms too small to see with just your eyes?

_____ _____ _____

Fungi

Mushrooms, molds, and yeasts are all organisms in the kingdom Fungi. Most fungi have cell walls like the cell walls of plants. Unlike plants, fungi do not use sunlight to make food. Fungi also do not "eat" the way that animals do. Instead, they use chemicals to break down food outside of their bodies. Then, they absorb, or take in, that food.

Mushrooms are in the kingdom Fungi.

 How do fungi "eat," or get the energy they need to live? _____

_____

Protists

Most protists are unicellular. Some are multicellular. The multicellular protists are too simple to be classified as animals, plants, or fungi. Seaweed is one example of a multicellular protist. All protists have complex cells with genetic material contained in a nucleus.

The kingdom Protista includes a wide variety of organisms. There are different groups of protists that evolved from different ancestors. In the future, the kingdom Protista may be divided into several groups.

Kelp, a type of seaweed, are multicellular protists.

Bacteria

Bacteria live nearly everywhere on Earth. There are more organisms in the Kingdom Bacteria than in any other kingdom.

All bacteria are unicellular. Their cells do not have a nucleus. Bacteria reproduce by dividing in two. They can produce many new organisms in a very short time.

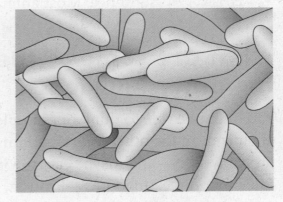

Bacteria are unicellular organisms with no nuclei.

Archaea

Like bacteria, archaea are unicellular organisms with no nucleus. Although archaea may seem similar to bacteria, their cell structure and genetic makeup are very different.

Archaea live in many different environments. Some archaea live in extreme environments. For example, some archaea live in very hot places, very cold places, and very salty places.

 How are archaea different from bacteria? _____

_____

Some members of Archaea live inside of volcanoes, near hot, liquid rock.

SECTION 7.3	
SUMMARIZE	**VOCABULARY**
1. List the kingdom or kingdoms that fit into each domain. **Bacteria:** _____ _____ _____ **Archaea:** _____ _____ _____ **Eukarya:** _____ _____ _____	Circle the correct term to answer each question. **2.** Which is the highest level of classification—**kingdom** or **domain?** **3.** Which is the term for animals that have backbones—**vertebrates** or **invertebrates?**

Review

CHAPTER

7 Classification of Living Things

CLASSZONE.COM
Go to ClassZone.com for activities, links, and more test practice.

Vocabulary

Circle the term that completes each sentence.

1 An insect is an example of a(n) **vertebrate / invertebrate**.

2 **Cladogram / Binomial nomenclature** is the system in which scientists give organisms two names.

3 A **domain / genus** is the highest level of classification.

4 A trait that has been changed through evolution is a **domain / derived characteristic**.

Reviewing Key Concepts

5 Look at the branching diagram. Which species share ancestor 1?

_____

6 What does each line on the branching diagram represent?

_____

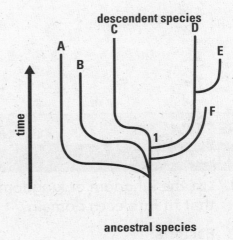

the BIG idea

7 What information is shown by a branching diagram, such as a cladogram?

_____

Test Practice

8 Scientist compare the visible traits of organisms to determine if they are related. What type of evidence is this?

A fossil evidence
B physical evidence
C genetic evidence
D menial evidence

9 What type of traits do scientists consider when making cladograms?

A derived characteristics
B acquired traits
C taxonomy
D binomial nomenclature

8 Systems in Organisms

the BIG idea

Organisms are made of different parts that work together to perform life functions.

Getting Ready to Learn

Review Concepts

- The cell is the basic unit of living things.
- Systems are made of interlocking parts that share matter and energy.
- Animals and plants belong to different kingdoms within the domain Eukarya.

Activity

How is a Bird Like a Frog? See student text, page 269.

Review Vocabulary

Explain the difference between each pair of words.

invertebrates and **vertebrates** _____

_____

unicellular and **multicellular** _____

_____

Preview Key Vocabulary

As you read the chapter, match each term in the box to the one it is most related to below. For each pair of words, tell why you put them together.

> organ
> exoskeleton
> shoot system

endoskeleton and _____

are a pair because _____

tissue and _____

are a pair because _____

root system and _____

are a pair because _____

8.1 Key Concept
Systems help organisms meet their needs.

 Student text pages 271–275

What do all living things have in common?

All living things have common needs. Organisms need energy, water and other materials, and a place to live. Different types of organisms meet these needs in different ways.

All organisms grow, respond to the environment, and reproduce. Organisms made of a single cell have all the structures they need to perform these activities of life. Multicellular organisms also have structures to perform these activities of life. In multicellular organisms, the structures are made of groups of specialized cells.

Activity

Specialization
See student text, page 272.

What are the different levels of organization for a multicellular organism?

Animals and plants are multicellular organisms. As animals and plants develop, their cells become specialized to do different jobs. For example, humans develop nerve cells, muscle cells, blood cells, and other types of cells. Cells become specialized through a process called differentiation. Cells of the same type do the same type of job.

Specialized Cells

muscle cell   nerve cell

Nerve cells and muscle cells are two types of specialized animal cells.

 Fill in the blank: As multicellular organisms develop, their cells _____.

Levels of Organization

The cells of a multicellular organism can be grouped in different ways. The way that cells are grouped is called levels of organization. There are five levels of organization: cells, tissues, organs, organ systems, and an organism.

 Fill in the blanks: What are the levels of organization, from smallest to largest? Cells, _____, _____, _____, whole organism.

You can see some of these levels of organization in the pictures.

1. The cell is the smallest level of organization.

2. A **tissue** is a group of many similar cells that work together. Muscle tissue is one type of tissue.

3. An **organ** is a group of two or more types of tissue that work together. The brain, lung, and heart are types of organs.

4. An **organ system** is a group of organs that work together. The digestive system includes organs and tissues in the mouth, stomach, intestines, and other places. They all work together to break down food.

5. The different levels all work together to keep an **organism** alive. If any part of the system fails,* it may cause an organ system to stop working. This could cause the organism to die.

 Circle the word or phrase that completes the sentence:
An organ system might fail if
only one / all of its parts fails.

Tissue

Muscle cells make up muscle tissue.

Organ

Muscles are organs made of muscle tissue.

Organ System

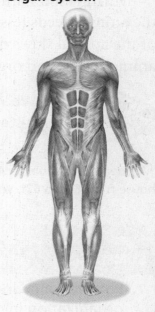

Many muscles make up the muscular system, an organ system.

*Academic Vocabulary: **Fail** means to stop working properly. If your bike's brakes **fail,** you will not be able to stop.

How do organs and systems respond to changes in the environment?

You might jump if you hear a loud noise or shiver if you are cold. Those are responses to your environment. Both animals and plants respond to the conditions in their environment. Systems and organs make adjustments* that help organisms meet their needs.

Plants Plants respond to light, gravity, moisture, temperature, and touch. For example, a plant will grow and bend toward light. Stems and leaves are plant organs that respond to changes in light.

Animals Animals also respond to their environment. In the winter, when there is less food, some animals hibernate. **Hibernation** is a sleeplike state that lasts for a long time. Bears may hibernate for as long as 100 days. Raccoons, hamsters, bats, and many other animals hibernate, too.

During hibernation, animals' organs slow down, so the animal needs less energy to survive. The heartbeat of the animal slows down. The chemical reactions in the animal's cells and organs also slow down.

Plants grow toward the Sun.

Mark It Up

Look at the picture. Where do you think the Sun would be? Draw it in.

INSTANT REPLAY What happens with the body systems of a hibernating animal?

_____

*Academic Vocabulary: **Adjustment** means a small change. If you change the temperature in your house from 66° to 67°, you've **adjusted** the temperature.

SECTION 8.1

SUMMARIZE	VOCABULARY
1. Put the following levels of organization in order from smallest to largest: *tissue, cell, organ system, whole organism, organ* _____ _____ _____	Fill in the blanks with the correct term. **hibernation** **tissue** **organ** 2. Body systems slow down for animals during _____. 3. The heart is an example of an _____. 4. A group of one type of cells that work together is called a _____.

Student text pages 277–283

What characteristics do plants have in common?

Plants live in many places on Earth, from deserts to tropical rain forests. There are many types of plants on Earth. All plants have several things in common.

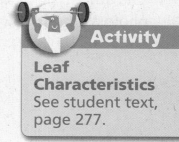

Activity

Leaf Characteristics See student text, page 277.

- Plants are multicellular.

- Plant cells have cell walls.

- Plants capture energy from the Sun through the process of photosynthesis.

What are three things that plants have in common?

_____

_____

What are the three types of plant tissue?

Like all multicellular organisms, plants have different levels of organization. They have cells that are grouped into tissues, tissues into organs, and organs into organ systems. Specialized plant cells form three types of tissues in plants—dermal tissue, vascular tissue, and ground tissue.

Dermal Tissue The tissue that covers a plant, like skin, is called dermal tissue. This tissue helps to protect the tissues underneath from injury or drying out. Plants get air through openings in the dermal tissue called stomata. **Stomata** allow water vapor, oxygen, and carbon dioxide to come in and out of the plant. Stomata can open to get carbon dioxide or let out oxygen. They close to stop water loss.

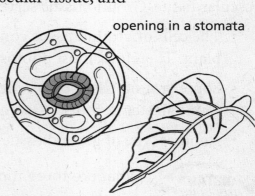

opening in a stomata

Stomata (blue) are openings in the dermal tissue of plants.

Vascular Tissue A second kind of tissue is called vascular (VAS-kyuh-lur) tissue. It is made of cells that carry water, nutrients, and sugars through a plant. In most plants, the **vascular system** is made up of two types of long, tubelike cells.

- One type carries water and nutrients from the roots to the leaves.
- The other type carries sugars and carbohydrates from photosynthesis down a stem and to the roots.

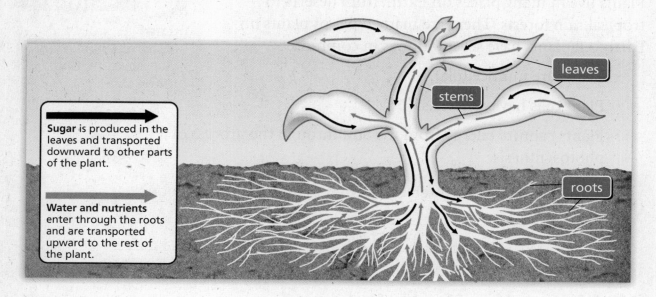

Sugar is produced in the leaves and transported downward to other parts of the plant.

Water and nutrients enter through the roots and are transported upward to the rest of the plant.

 What does vascular tissue do? _____

_____

Ground Tissue Most of a plant is made up of ground tissue. It is the tissue in all parts of the plant, between the dermal tissue and the vascular tissue. Ground tissue serves three main functions.

- The cells of ground tissue contain most of the chloroplasts in a plant. Therefore, most photosynthesis happens in ground tissue.
- Some ground tissue cells store sugars and starches. This tissue is found in stems, roots, fruits, and seeds.
- Another type of ground tissue cells hold the plant up off the ground.

 What are three functions of ground tissue?

_____

_____

How do plant tissues work together in systems?

Plant tissues are organized into three main organs—roots, stems, and leaves. These organs make up two organ systems: the shoot system and the root system. The shoot system and root system are both part of the vascular system.

Activity

Roots
See student text, page 280.

What are three main plant organs?

_____ _____ _____

The Shoot System

Stems and leaves make up the **shoot system,** which is where photosynthesis happens and where the plant exchanges materials with the air. The shoot system also helps hold a plant up. The stems of some plants can store sugars in the form of starch. Potatoes, taro, yams, garlic, and onions are all types of modified stems.

The Root System

The **root system** is below the ground. It holds a plant in place and lets a plant take up water and nutrients from the soil. Roots can also store sugars made through photosynthesis in the form of starch. Beets, turnips, and carrots are examples of root storage structures.

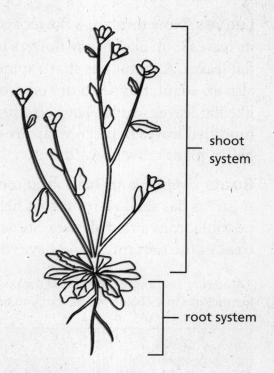

shoot system

root system

The shoot system and the root system are two main plant organ systems.

System Failure

Damage to any part of the plant can affect the entire organism. Damaged roots may not be able to absorb enough water and nutrients to keep a plant healthy. Damaged shoots may not be able to use photosynthesis to get energy. A healthy plant can repair small wounds and survive. A weakened plant may not be able to survive damage.

What are some plant adaptations for different environments?

Most plants have similar tissues that make up their organs. But different plants have different types of stems, leaves, and roots. These different kinds of organs are adaptations for different environments.

This cactus has several adapations.

Stems Imagine a tall flower. It probably has a long, thin stem. Now look at the cactus in the picture. Desert plants, such as the cactus, often have thick stems that store water. This is an adaptation to a dry environment.

Leaves Now think of a flower again. What do its leaves look like? Many flowers have wide and flat leaves. A cactus has sharp spines that are modified* leaves. This is also an adaptation for a dry environment. The spines do not dry out like flat leaves would. They also protect the plant. Some plants have modified leaves that can wrap around other plants or structures, and help a plant grow upward.

Roots Some plants have deep roots, and others have shallow roots. A cactus has shallow roots that help quickly absorb as much water as possible from a rain shower. Some plants grow on the trunks of tall trees in the rain forest and have roots that never touch the soil.

*Academic Vocabulary: **Modified** means different from an earlier form. If you follow all of the instructions in a cookie recipe, but you add more nuts, you have **modified** the recipe.

SECTION 8.2

SUMMARIZE	VOCABULARY
1. Like animals, plants have tissues, organs, and organ systems. Give one example of each. Tissues: _____ Organs: _____ Organ Systems: _____ _____	Draw a line to connect each term to its definition. **2.** root system **a.** openings that let a plant take in and release gases **3.** shoot system **b.** takes in water and nutrients **4.** stomata **c.** where photosynthesis happens

SECTION 8.3

Key Concept

Animals have several levels of organization.

Student text pages 285–291

What do all animals have in common?

A huge variety of animals live on Earth. Although there are many different types of animals, they have several things in common.

- Animals are multicelluar.
- Animal cells do not have cell walls.
- Animals get energy from eating other organisms.

Activity

Animal Movement
See student text, page 285.

What are three things that animals have in common?

_____

What are the four types of animal tissues?

Like plants, animal cells are organized into tissues, organs, and organ systems. Most animals have only four different types of tissues: epithelial tissue, nerve tissue, muscle tissue, and connective tissue.

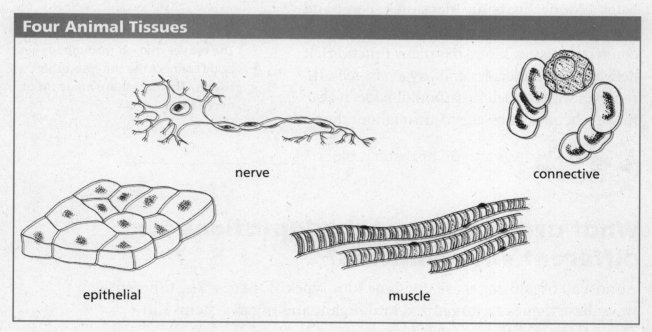

Four Animal Tissues

nerve

connective

epithelial

muscle

Epithelial Tissue The skin that covers the outside of most animals is epithelial tissue (EHP-uh-THEE-lee-uhl). The lining of structures such as the mouth, stomach, and intestines is also epithelial tissue. This tissue protects the animal's organs. It also lets materials be absorbed, or taken in, and secreted, or moved out.

 Which type of tissue is the skin surface?

_____

Nerve Tissue Many body activities are controlled by nerve tissue. This tissue sends electrical signals through the body. In animals with backbones, the brain, spinal cord, and nerves are made of nerve tissue. Other animals, such as sea stars, do not have a brain. Instead they have a net of nerve tissues.

Muscle Tissue Movement is made possible by muscle tissue. Muscle tissue lets animals run, jump, swim, and wiggle. Movement inside animals' bodies, such as the beating of the heart, also happens through muscle tissue.

Connective Tissue Body parts are joined together by connective tissue. Tendons are connective tissues that connect muscle with bone. Fat is a connective tissue that stores energy and gives padding to some organs. Blood is also a connective tissue. Blood has many functions. It delivers food molecules and oxygen to cells. It removes wastes, such as carbon dioxide. It also moves chemical messengers throughout the body.

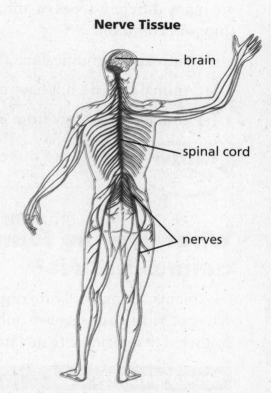

Nerve Tissue

brain

spinal cord

nerves

The nerves that go throughout your body connect the brain to other tissues. The nerves are made up of nerve tissue.

 What type of tissue is blood? _____

What are some animal adaptations for different environments?

Almost all organisms share the same four types of tissues. The different ways these tissues are organized into organs and organ systems show adaptations to different environments.

Eyes The organs that respond to light are called eyes. Eyes are part of an animal's nervous system. Different organisms have different types of eyes, adapted to different environments. Some organisms, such as worms and sea stars, just have groups of nerves that can sense light. Insects have eyes with many tiny lenses that allow the animal to see in all directions at once. Octopus, squid, and most vertebrates have eyes that can focus and provide sharp images.

Skin All four types of tissue make up the organ called skin. Skin provides protection and support. It also helps an animal control its body temperature. Different types of skin have different adaptations. Mammal skin produces hair. Bird skin produces feathers. Fish skin produces scales.

Skeletal Systems Vertebrates are organisms with backbones, and invertebrates are organisms without backbones. The skeletal system of vertebrates is called an endoskeleton. An **endoskeleton** is under the skin. It has bones, cartilage, ligaments, and tendons. Invertebrates such as crabs, shrimp, and insects do not have bones or other parts of an internal skeleton. Instead, many invertebrates have an **exoskeleton,** an outer covering that supports and protects the animal. You can see both types of skeletal systems in the pictures below.

Skeletal Systems

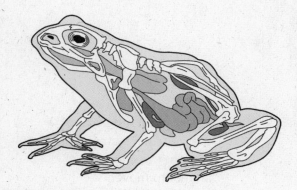

Vertebrates have an **endoskeleton.**

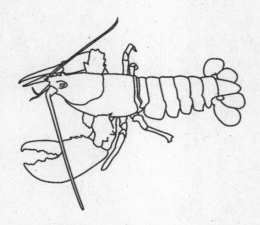

Lobsters and many other invertebrates have an **exoskeleton.**

What is the difference between an endoskeleton and an exoskeleton? _____

_____

How do some organ systems work together in humans?

Almost all animals have organ systems. Many organ systems work together to make up a whole organism. Here's how some organ systems work together in humans.

Respiratory and Circulatory Systems The respiratory and circulatory systems work together to get oxygen into the body. They also help release carbon dioxide. The respiratory system takes in or removes gases. The circulatory system moves gases through the body.

Skeletal and Muscular Systems The skeletal and muscular systems also work together. The skeletal system includes the bones in your body. It supports your weight and protects your organs. The muscular system and the skeletal system help you move. Muscles pull parts of a skeleton. When muscles pull on bones, the bones move.

Skeletal System

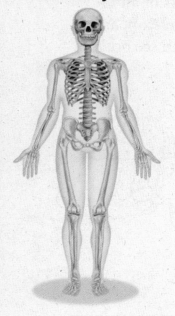

Muscular System

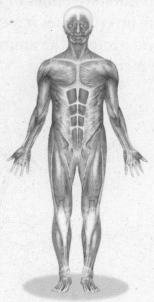

Visual Connection
See how bones and muscles are connected in student text, page 289.

The skeletal system and the muscular system work together to allow an animal to move.

How do muscles move bones? _____

_____

In addition to these four systems, there are many others. For example, the digestive system processes the food and liquids an animal eats. The urinary system removes wastes from blood and releases them in urine. The nervous system lets an animal respond to the world around it and connects the systems of the body together. These and other organ systems all work together in an organism.

INSTANT REPLAY What is the digestive system? _____
_____

SECTION 8.3

SUMMARIZE	VOCABULARY
1. Name at least two animal organ systems. _____ _____ _____ _____ _____	Fill in the blanks to complete the sentences. **exoskeleton** **endoskeleton** 2. Crabs, insects, and many other invertebrates have _____. 3. Humans, fish, frogs, and other vertebrates have _____.

Student text pages
294–301

Are your organ systems always active?

Even during sleep, your organ systems are working. The body's systems are always active. The body needs to breathe and circulate blood all the time. The cells, tissues, organs, and organ systems work to keep a person alive. If one part of the body fails, a person could get sick or die.

Activity

Exercise
See student text, page 295.

What is homeostasis?

Homeostasis (HOH-mee-oh-STAY-sihs) is the body's ability to keep its internal* conditions within normal ranges. For example, your body's normal internal temperature is about 37°C (98°–99°F). Even if it is hotter or colder outside, your body stays about the same temperature. This is because your systems respond to cool you down when you get hot and warm you up when you get cold.

If an organ or tissue fails, the body might not be able to maintain homeostasis. Then all the other organ systems might fail too.

What is homeostasis? Underline the sentence that tells you.

How does the endocrine system help maintain homeostasis?

Maintaining homeostasis is a very important function of the endocrine system. The endocrine system controls conditions in the body by making and releasing chemicals that move throughout the body. These chemicals are called hormones.

Visual Connection

See the location of the glands that make up the endocrine system in the student text, page 299.

*Academic Vocabulary: **Internal** means inside. An **internal** wall in a building is not connected to the outside.

Hormones are chemicals that are made in specialized tissues. They travel through the blood and cause certain cells to change their activity. Hormones are made in specialized tissues called **glands.** Many glands in different parts of the body produce hormones.

Here is how the endocrine system helps maintain homeostasis. If the body's conditions change, homeostasis is disrupted. Glands respond by making and releasing hormones. The hormones move throughout the body. They cause certain cells to act differently to help bring the body's conditions back to normal. In this way, homeostasis is maintained.

 How are glands and hormones related?

_____

What happens when homeostasis is disrupted?

Hormones from the endocrine system help your body maintain homeostasis. But homeostasis can be disrupted. When this happens, it can cause problems with a person's health.

If a gland makes too much or too little of a hormone it can cause disease. For example, diabetes is a disease that can happen if a gland called the pancreas cannot make hormones that help balance the levels of sugar in your blood. Diseases can also cause other organs to fail. For example, diabetes can lead to heart disease, blindness, and kidney damage.

 What do hormones have to do with diabetes?

_____

SECTION 8.4	
SUMMARIZE	**VOCABULARY**
1. What is the relationship between homeostasis and health? _____ _____ _____	Draw a line to connect each word to its definition. 2. homeostasis a. chemicals made by glands 3. hormones b. tissues of the endocrine system 4. glands c. balanced internal conditions

Review

CHAPTER 8 Systems in Organisms

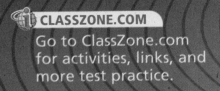

CLASSZONE.COM
Go to ClassZone.com
for activities, links, and
more test practice.

Vocabulary Circle the correct word or words to answer each question.

1 What is a tissue made of—**a group of similar cells** or **organs?**

2 In which plant organ system does photosynthesis happen—
the root system or **the shoot system?**

3 What type of skeletal system do dogs, birds, and other
vertebrates have—**an endoskeleton** or **an exoskeleton?**

4 What animal structures make and release hormones—**glands** or **stomata?**

Reviewing Key Concepts

5 What are the levels of organization in plants and animals?

_____

6 How do your skeletal and muscular systems work together to
allow you to move?

_____

7 How does homeostasis keep organ systems from failing?

_____

the BIG idea

8 Suppose an organ is made up of three tissues. What will happen to this
organ if one of the tissues fails? What will happen to the organ system?

_____

Test Practice

9 Which three parts make up an organ
system?

   A organs, tissues, and cells
   B cells, hormones, and connective
     tissue
   C genus, phylum, and order
   D dermal, vascular, and muscle tissue

10 Blood, tendons, and fat are
types of

   A organ systems
   B organs
   C muscles
   D connective tissue

CHAPTER
9 Reproduction

the **BIG** idea

Reproductive systems allow the production of offspring.

Getting Ready to Learn

Review Concepts

- Both sexual and asexual reproduction involve cell division.

- Meiosis is a special form of cell division.

- Organisms inherit DNA from their parents.

Activity

What's Inside a Chicken Egg?
See student text, page 311.

Review Vocabulary

Draw a line to connect each word to its definition.

mitosis   a female gamete

egg   cell division that results in egg or sperm

sperm   cell division that results in two identical cells

meiosis   a male gamete

Preview Key Vocabulary

Here are some terms you will learn in this chapter. As you read the chapter, complete each sentence to explain how the terms are related. Write your sentences below.

An embryo _____ uterus.

An embryo _____ seed.

Sperm _____ egg.

SECTION
9.1
Key Concept
Organisms reproduce in different ways.

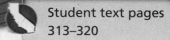
Student text pages
313–320

What are some different types of asexual reproduction?

Organisms must reproduce to make more organisms. There are two types of reproduction: asexual and sexual reproduction. Asexual reproduction involves only one parent. Sexual reproduction involves two parents.

 Fill in the blanks: Asexual reproduction requires _____ parent(s), but sexual reproduction requires _____ parent(s).

Many organisms, including bacteria, plants, and many invertebrates, reproduce asexually. But only one vertebrate—a type of lizard—can reproduce asexually. Other vertebrates do not reproduce asexually.

There are several different ways that organisms can reproduce asexually.

Binary Fission Many single-celled organisms, such as bacteria, reproduce through cell division that results in two identical cells. This process is called binary fission.

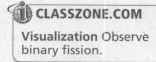
CLASSZONE.COM
Visualization Observe binary fission.

Budding Some organisms, such as jellyfish and yeast, can reproduce through a process called budding. The parent grows a small bud or branch that later separates and forms a new individual.

Regeneration Other organisms, such as flatworms, some plants, and some fungi, can reproduce by breaking into two pieces. Each piece then grows back all of the necessary parts and becomes a complete organism.

The offspring of asexual reproduction are genetically the same as the parent.

 Which types of animals—vertebrates or invertebrates—are more likely to reproduce asexually?

_____

What is sexual reproduction?

Sexual reproduction happens in vertebrates, plants, and fungi. Sexual reproduction involves two parents. Offspring that are produced sexually get half of their DNA from each parent.

Before sexual reproduction, each parent makes cells with half the normal amount of DNA. These cells are called **gametes.** Males and females have different types of gametes. Gametes produced by males are called sperm. Gametes produced by females are called eggs.

When the male and female gametes join, they produce an offspring with the normal amount of DNA. The process of gametes joining and combining their DNA is called **fertilization.** Fertilization produces a zygote. A **zygote** is a fertilized egg. It has a complete set of DNA—half a set from each parent—and will develop into a mature individual.

Eggs and sperm are **gametes.**

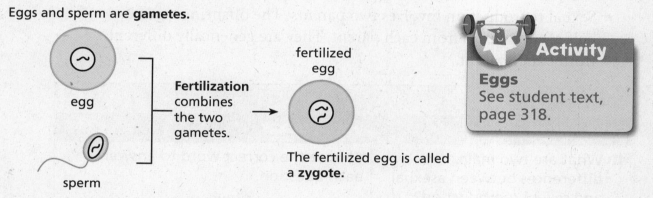

egg

sperm

Fertilization combines the two gametes.

fertilized egg

The fertilized egg is called a **zygote.**

Activity

Eggs
See student text, page 318.

Sexual Reproduction in Animals

In some animals, eggs are fertilized inside the female's body. In other animals, the eggs are fertilized outside the female's body. Most animals that live in water fertilize eggs outside the female's body. First, the female lays eggs in the water. Then, the male releases sperm nearby.

The eggs of humans and many other animals are fertilized inside the female's body. Some animals, such as birds and reptiles, lay the fertilized eggs in a nest. The offspring of most mammals, including humans, develop inside the mother's body after fertilization.

What are two different ways that animal eggs may be fertilized?

_____

_____

Sexual Reproduction in Plants and Bacteria

Some plants have both male and female parts on the same plant. They can produce sperm cells that fertilize their own eggs.

Many bacteria and other single-celled organisms can exchange DNA. These organisms are not males or females. However, certain cells can pass DNA through a bridge-like structure that connects to another cell.

How do asexual and sexual reproduction compare?

Asexual reproduction and sexual reproduction differ in a number of ways.

- Asexual reproduction involves one parent. The offspring are genetically identical to the parent.

- Sexual reproduction involves two parents. The offspring receive half of their genes from each parent. They are genetically different from either parent.

SECTION 9.1	
SUMMARIZE	**VOCABULARY**
1. What are two main differences between asexual and sexual reproduction? _____ _____ _____ _____ _____ _____	Choose the correct word to answer each question. **gamete fertilization zygote** 2. What is a fertilized egg? _____ 3. What type of cell are eggs and sperm? _____ 4. What is the joining of an egg and sperm? _____

SECTION 9.2 Key Concept
Plants can reproduce in several ways.

Student text pages 322–329

How do plants reproduce asexually?

Have you ever noticed a potato or onion in your kitchen that started sprouting? This is a form of asexual reproduction called vegetative propagation. **Vegetative propagation** (PRAHP-uh-GAY-shuhn) is a form of asexual reproduction in which new plants grow from stems, leaves, roots, and other non-reproductive tissues. Many plants reproduce both sexually and asexually.

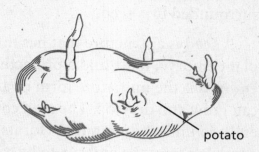

potato

Vegetative propagation occurs when new plants grow from stems, leaves, roots, or other non-reproductive organs.

Is vegetative propagation a form of sexual or asexual reproduction?

How do plants reproduce sexually?

Some plants, such as mosses and ferns, need water to reproduce. The sperm of these plants can only move through water. The sperm travels through the water in puddles and moist* ground to reach the eggs. These plants are adapted to moist habitats.

Activity

Fruit
See student text, page 322.

Other plants do not need water for sexual reproduction. Seeds and pollen are two important adaptations that allow some plants to live in drier habitats.

*Academic Vocabulary: **Moist** means a little wet. If you walk on wet grass with a hole in your shoes, your socks might get **moist**.

A **pollen** grain is a dry structure that holds a sperm cell and another cell that helps the sperm travel to the egg. The pollen grain protects the sperm from drying out. Pollen is carried by wind, water, or animals. A pollen grain attaches to the part of a plant that contains the egg and releases its sperm. Fertilization occurs and produces an embryo that is surrounded by a seed.

A **seed** is a structure that has three parts—a plant embryo, food, and a protective coat. An **embryo** is the immature form of an organism that can grow and develop. The seed coat protects the embryo until the conditions for its survival are good. It allows the embryo to be carried by wind, animals, or water. Seeds can travel very far and survive harsh conditions.

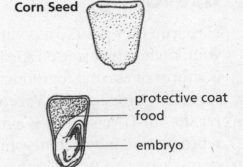

Corn Seed

protective coat
food

embryo

What are three parts of a seed?

_____ _____ _____

What are the reproductive organs of plants?

All plants produce seeds. But only some plants can produce fruits. Plants that produce fruits are called flowering plants. Most of the plants you know are flowering plants. Roses, daisies, oak trees, corn, beans, and grass are all flowering plants. The reproductive organ of a flowering plant is the flower. It has two main reproductive structures: a pistil and many stamen.

These flowers are the reproductive organs of this cherry blossom.

Pistil The pistil is the female reproductive structure, shown in the picture below. An ovary is at the bottom of the pistil. The ovary contains at least one **ovule** that holds an immature egg cell. After the egg cell is fertilized, an embryo grows inside the ovule.

Stamen The stamen is the male reproductive structure, shown in the picture. The stamen is made up of an anther that sits atop a filament. The anther makes sperm cells. The sperm cells are inside grains of pollen. The pollen travels by wind, water, or animals to the pistil to fertilize the egg.

Mark It Up

Write *egg* over the plant structure that makes eggs and *sperm* over the structure that makes sperm.

Reproductive Parts of a Flower

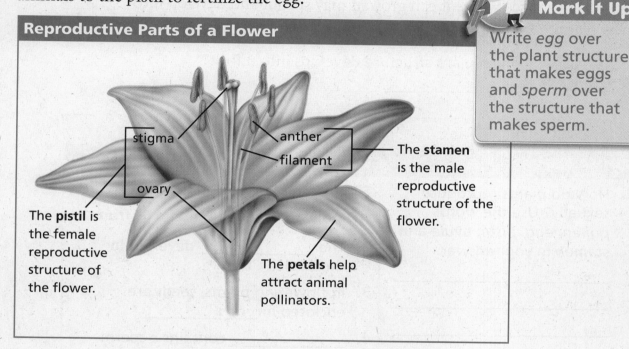

stigma

anther

filament

ovary

The **pistil** is the female reproductive structure of the flower.

The **stamen** is the male reproductive structure of the flower.

The **petals** help attract animal pollinators.

The color, size, shape, and smell of the flower are adaptations that help attract animals to the plant. Animals may help move the pollen from the stamen of one plant to the pistil of another.

In which plant reproductive structure are eggs found?

_____

A **fruit** is a mature plant ovary. Apples and figs are plant ovaries. These fruits have many seeds. Other fruits, such as cherries, have only one seed. Walnuts, almonds, and other nuts are also plant ovaries.

Now that you have read about the different plant parts, let's think about the whole life cycle of a flowering plant.

Visual Connection

See the Life Cycle of a Cherry Tree in the student text, page 328.

Meiosis takes place in the flowers of a plant to produce sperm and eggs. The sperm is contained within pollen. Pollen may travel by wind, water, or animals to the pistil of another flower.

The pollen grain produces a tube that grows into the pistil. The sperm cell moves through the tube and fertilizes the egg cell in the ovule. The fertilized egg grows into an embryo. The ovary develops into a fruit that contains seeds.

The fruit may fall to the ground or be eaten by an animal. If the seed falls in a place where it can grow, it may sprout and develop into a new plant.

 Which plant structure develops into a fruit?

_____

SECTION 9.2	
SUMMARIZE	**VOCABULARY**
1. How do plants reproduce sexually? Use the words *pollen, egg, pistil, ovule* and *stamen* in your answer. _____ _____ _____ _____ _____ _____	Fill in each blank with the correct word. **pollen seed embryo fruit** 2. The _____ develops in the ovule. 3. In flowering plants, seeds are enclosed in _____. 4. _____ contains a sperm cell. 5. The _____ has an embryo, food, and protective coat.

Key Concept

Human reproduction is a complex process.

Student text pages
332–340

What are the parts of the human reproductive system?

Just like in plants, the human reproductive gametes are sperm and eggs. Sperm cells contain genetic material from the male. Egg cells have genetic material from the female.

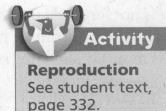

Activity

Reproduction
See student text, page 332.

The Female Reproductive System

The female reproductive system has two functions. One function is to make egg cells. The second function is to protect and feed the developing offspring until birth. There are many parts to the female reproductive system.

Eggs are produced in the ovaries. Females have two ovaries. The ovaries are on either side of a larger organ called the uterus. The uterus is where the offspring develops until birth. You can see the ovaries, uterus, and other parts of the female reproductive system in the picture.

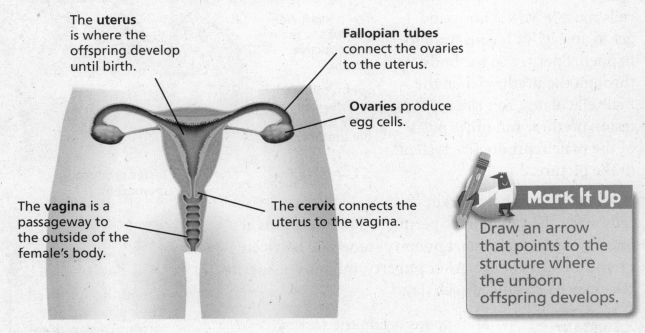

The **uterus** is where the offspring develop until birth.

Fallopian tubes connect the ovaries to the uterus.

Ovaries produce egg cells.

The **vagina** is a passageway to the outside of the female's body.

The **cervix** connects the uterus to the vagina.

Mark It Up

Draw an arrow that points to the structure where the unborn offspring develops.

INSTANT REPLAY

What are two roles of the female reproductive system?

_____   _____

A human female is born with thousands of egg cells. The egg cells cannot be fertilized until the female reaches puberty. In humans, most females start puberty sometime between 10 and 14 years of age.

At puberty, eggs begin to develop. The uterus lining thickens with blood. The thick lining gets the uterus ready in case the egg is fertilized. One ovary will release one egg each month—about every 28 days. If the egg is not fertilized, the egg and the spongy lining of the uterus begin to break down. The lining of the uterus exits the body through the vagina. This monthly shedding of the uterus lining is called **menstruation.**

 After puberty, how often do the ovaries release an egg?

_____

The Male Reproductive System

The functions of the male reproductive system are to produce sperm and to deliver sperm to the female reproductive system. Sperm cells are produced in the testis. Males have two testes. Sperm cells must leave the body and get to an egg for fertilization to happen. Sperm exit the body through the urethra when the male ejaculates. You can see the testes, urethra, and other parts of the male reproductive system in the picture.

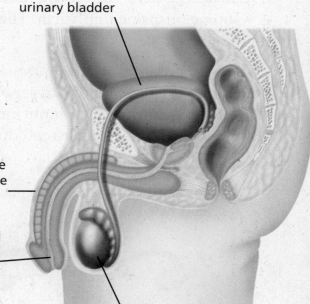

urinary bladder

The **penis** is one part of the male reproductive system.

Sperm cells and urine exit the body through the **urethra.**

Testes produce sperm cells.

Males do not have sperm cells when they are born. Sperm production begins at puberty. Most males start puberty sometime between 11 and 14 years of age. After puberty, millions of sperm cells may be produced each day.

 What happens inside the testes?

_____

Mark It Up

Circle the name of the reproductive organ of the male where sperm are made.

How do humans produce offspring?

The production of offspring includes sexual intercourse, fertilization, pregnancy, and birth. Sexual intercourse is the act in which the male inserts his penis into the female's vagina and ejaculates. Ejaculation releases millions of sperm cells. The sperm swim into the uterus. If a sperm reaches an egg, fertilization may occur.

Fertilization

Fertilization is the joining of the sperm and egg cell. The DNA of the sperm combines with the DNA of the egg. The fertilized egg, or zygote, begins dividing. Once the egg begins to divide, and until eight weeks after fertilization, the developing organism is called an embryo.

CLASSZONE.COM

Visualization Follow an egg from fertilization to implantation.

About one week after fertilization, the embryo attaches itself to the thickened lining of the uterus. After the embryo attaches, the mother's body goes through many chemical changes to prepare for the next stage—pregnancy.

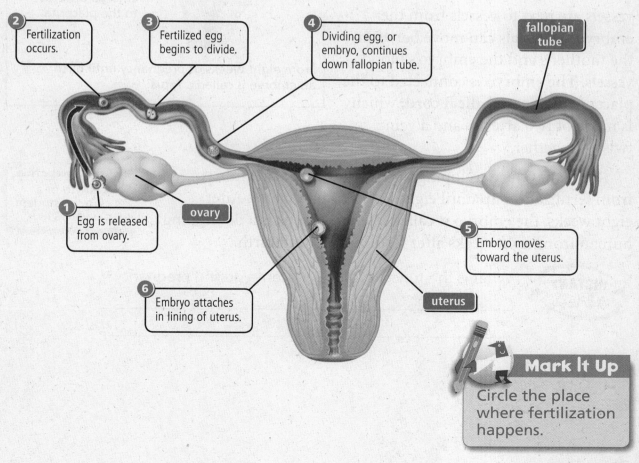

2 Fertilization occurs.

3 Fertilized egg begins to divide.

4 Dividing egg, or embryo, continues down fallopian tube.

fallopian tube

1 Egg is released from ovary.

ovary

5 Embryo moves toward the uterus.

6 Embryo attaches in lining of uterus.

uterus

Mark It Up

Circle the place where fertilization happens.

Fertilization does not always occur. But there is always a chance that fertilization will happen after sexual intercourse. Every time a male and a female have sex, there is a chance that the female will become pregnant, even if birth control is used.

 When might fertilization occur? _____

_____

Pregnancy

Human pregnancy lasts nine months. In the first week after the embryo attaches to the uterus, the embryo grows rapidly. A new organ forms. This organ is called the placenta.

The **placenta** is an organ that gets nutrients to the embryo and takes away wastes. The placenta is filled with blood vessels. The mother's blood vessels are next to vessels from the embryo. Materials can move between the mother's and the embryo's blood vessels. The embryo is connected to the placenta by the **umbilical cord,** which is made of two arteries and a vein twisted together.

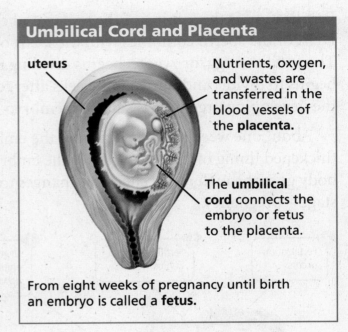

Umbilical Cord and Placenta

uterus

Nutrients, oxygen, and wastes are transferred in the blood vessels of the **placenta.**

The **umbilical cord** connects the embryo or fetus to the placenta.

From eight weeks of pregnancy until birth an embryo is called a **fetus.**

Recall that the developing organism is called an embryo from fertilization up until eight weeks of pregnancy. After eight weeks, the embryo is called a fetus. A **fetus** is a developing human from eight weeks after fertilization until birth.

Visual Connection
See Growth of a Fetus in the student text, page 339.

 What is the function of the placenta during pregnancy?

_____

_____

Labor and Delivery

After nine months, the fetus is grown and ready to leave the mother's body. There are three main parts of birth: labor, delivery of the fetus, and delivery of the placenta.

Labor begins with strong muscle movements of the uterus called contractions. At first, the contractions happen about every 15 to 30 minutes. With each contraction, the cervix widens. Over time, the contractions happen more and more frequently. When contractions happen about every two minutes, the cervix is wide enough for the fetus to pass through.

Then, the mother's muscles push the fetus out of the uterus and through the vagina. After delivery, the umbilical cord is cut. After the cord is cut, the fetus becomes a separate individual. Finally, the placenta is delivered, and the process of birth is complete.

What is the first part in the process of birth?

_____

SECTION 9.3

SUMMARIZE	VOCABULARY
1. Where does the embryo of each of the following organisms grow after fertilization? Flowering plants: _____ Humans: _____	Write each term next to its description. **fertilization placenta umbilical cord** 2. Blood vessels that connect a fetus to the mother _____ 3. Organ that exchanges nutrients and wastes between a mother and an embryo or fetus _____ 4. Combining of a sperm and egg _____

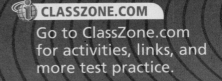

Vocabulary Describe the relationship between each pair of words below.

1 **fetus** and **uterus** _____

2 **plant embryo** and **seed** _____

3 **placenta** and **umbilical cord** _____

Reviewing Key Concepts

4 Fill in the chart below to compare sexual and asexual reproduction.

Type of Reproduction	How many parent organisms are involved—one or two?	Are the offspring genetically identical or different?	Which of the following organisms can reproduce this way—bacteria, plants, vertebrates?
Asexual Reproduction			
Sexual Reproduction			

5 What are the two main reproductive organs of a flowering plant?

_____

the BIG idea

6 What is the main role of the ovaries and the testes in humans?

_____

Test Practice

7 Which part of a flower contains the egg?

A pollen
B anther
C pistil
D seed

8 Which word refers to the process of an egg and sperm joining?

A fertilization
B contractions
C stamen
D embryo

CHAPTER
10 Movement and Forces

the BIG idea

Muscles and bones provide forces and levers to move the body.

Getting Ready to Learn

Review Concepts

- The cell is the basic unit of living things.
- Systems in living things are made up of interacting parts that share matter and energy.
- In multicellular organisms, cells work together to support life.

Activity

How Many Bones Are in Your Hand?
See student text, page 347.

Review Vocabulary

Fill in the blanks to complete the sentences below.

1. The body is made of _____, tissues, organs, and organ _____.

2. _____ is the ability of the body to maintain internal conditions within a normal range.

Preview Key Vocabulary

As you read the chapter, fill in the concept map below.

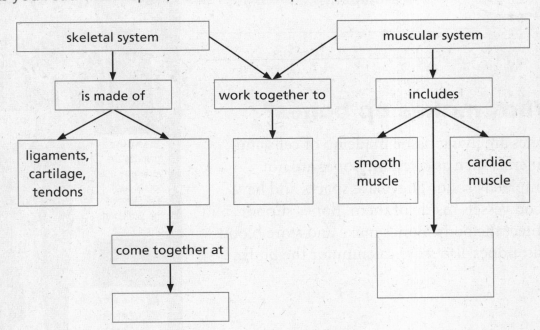

Student text pages
349–355

What is the skeletal system?

The **skeletal system** is made up of bones, ligaments, cartilage, and tendons. Like the frame of a building, the skeleton gives the body shape. Your body can move because of the way muscles work with the skeletal system. The skeletal system also protects the organs inside your body.

The skeleton has two main parts: the axial (AK-see-uhl) skeleton and the appendicular (AP-uhn-DIHK-yuh-luhr) skeleton. The **axial skeleton** is the center part of the skeleton that includes the skull, spinal column, and the ribs. This part of the skeleton mainly provides support and protection. The **appendicular skeleton** includes the arms, legs, and other bones that work to let the body move.

What are two parts of the skeletal system?

_____

_____

What makes up bones?

Bones are living tissue made up of cells and minerals such as calcium. Bones are not completely solid. They have spaces and have blood vessels inside of them. Bones support and protect the body. Bones make and store blood cells. Bones also store calcium for the body.

CLASSZONE.COM

Simulation Assemble a virtual skeleton.

Mark It Up

Circle the names of three bones that are part of the axial skeleton.

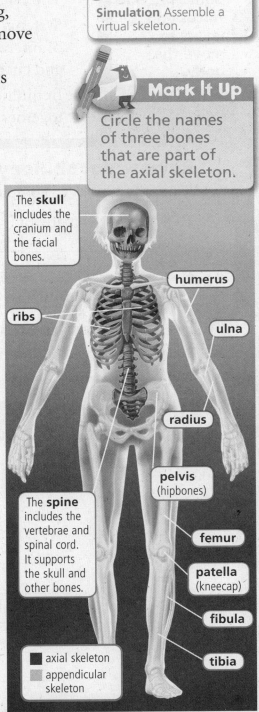

The **skull** includes the cranium and the facial bones.

humerus

ribs

ulna

radius

pelvis (hipbones)

The **spine** includes the vertebrae and spinal cord. It supports the skull and other bones.

femur

patella (kneecap)

fibula

tibia

■ axial skeleton
□ appendicular skeleton

What are the different kinds of joints that connect the skeletal system?

A **joint** is a place where two bones in the skeletal system meet. Joints let the body move. There are different kinds of joints. Some joints allow for more movement than other joints.

The bones inside the skull are connected by joints that do not move at all. There is no space between these bones. Your ribs are connected to a central bone by joints that move a tiny bit. There is no space between the bones, but they can move a little because they are connected by cartilage. **Cartilage** (KAHR-tl-ihj) is a tough but flexible connective tissue. The outermost part of your ear is also a type of cartilage.

 Do all joints allow for movement? Explain.

_____

Most of the joints in your body move freely. The bones of moveable joints are separated by a space that contains fluid. You will read more about fluids in Chapter 11.

Moveable joints move in different ways. Your shoulder, for example, moves differently than does your knee. Both of those body parts move differently than your thumb moves. You can compare the different ways that joints move to the different movements of simple devices. Some examples are described below.

Hinge Joint Your elbows and knees are hinge joints. You can bend and straighten these joints, like a hinge that allows you to open and close a door.

Pivot Joint Your elbow also has a pivot joint. This allows you to twist, or pivot, your arm as if you were turning a doorknob.

Ball-and-Socket Joint Your shoulder and hip have ball-and-socket joints. This type of joint lets you swing your arm or leg in many directions.

 What kind of joints are found at the knees?

Activity

Movable Joints
See student text, page 353.

Visual Connection
See joints in the student text, page 354.

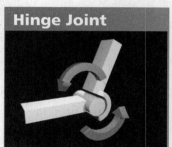

Hinge Joint

Your elbows and knees are hinge joints.

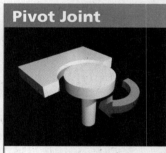

Pivot Joint

Your elbow also has a pivot joint.

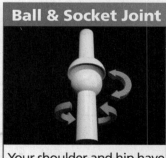

Ball & Socket Joint

Your shoulder and hip have ball-and-socket joints.

Gliding Joint Some small, flat bones in your ankles and wrists can slide or glide over one another. The vertebrae in your spine move by gliding joints. These joints give a little movement.

Visual Connection
See joints in the student text, page 355.

Saddle Joint Only the thumb has a saddle joint. This joint allows back-and-forth, side-to-side, and circular movement.

Ellipsoid Joint These joints connect your fingers to the rest of your hand. Ellipsoid joints let the bones move like a hinge in many directions. But these joints cannot rotate, or twist.

Gliding Joint	Saddle Joint	Ellipsoid Joint
		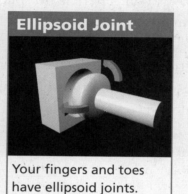
Some joints in your ankles and wrists are gliding joints.	The only saddle joint in your body is at the base of your thumb.	Your fingers and toes have ellipsoid joints.

 Where in your body can you find a saddle joint?

_____

SECTION 10.1

SUMMARIZE

1. The knee is a hinge joint and the shoulder is a ball-and-socket joint. Use two or three sentences to describe how the movement of the knee joint differs from the movement of the shoulder joint.

_____

_____

_____

_____

VOCABULARY

Draw a line to connect each word to its definition.

2. skeletal system   a. where two bones meet

3. joint   b. the knee or elbow

4. cartilage   c. body's framework

5. hinge joint   d. tough, flexible tissue

Student text pages
356–362

What are three functions of muscles?

Muscles are organs that produce all of the movement in your body. Muscles make the heart beat, the eyes blink, and every other body movement happen. Muscles also help keep your body temperature at a normal level and help you maintain your posture.* The **muscular system** is the system of all the muscles in your body. The three functions of muscles are described below.

Movement Skeletal muscles are muscles that are attached to the bones in your body. Most skeletal muscles are attached to bones by tendons. Together, bones and muscles allow you to move.

Activity

Muscles
See student text, page 356.

Maintaining Body Temperature Your body must stay within a normal temperature range. When your body gets cold, muscles make your body shiver. The muscle movement that makes you shiver also gives off heat. This helps to raise your body temperature.

Maintaining Posture Most muscles in your body are always a little bit active. Try balancing on one leg. You can feel different muscles working to keep you balanced. You don't have to think about which muscles to use; it just happens.

Circle three functions of muscles listed above.

What are three different types of muscles in your body?

Your body has three types of muscles. These muscle types do different things and are found in different parts of the body. All types of muscles work the same way. All muscles contract and relax. When they contract, the muscle cells get shorter. When muscle cells relax, they get longer. The three different types of muscles are skeletal muscle, smooth muscle, and cardiac muscle.

*Academic Vocabulary: **Posture** means the position of the body. When you stand up straight, your **posture** lets you walk with a book balanced on top of your head.

Skeletal Muscle The muscle tissue that is attached to bones in the body is called **skeletal muscle.** You control the movement of your skeletal muscles. Turning your head, raising your arm, and wiggling your toes are movements of skeletal muscles.

Smooth Muscle Not all muscles are attached to bones. **Smooth muscle** is a type of muscle that attaches to organs in your body, and it works without your control. This type of muscle is found in the walls of organs, such as the stomach and intestines. Smooth muscle pushes food through the digestive system. Smooth muscle is also found around blood vessels. It controls how wide your blood vessels are.

Cardiac Muscle Your heart is made of **cardiac muscle.** Like smooth muscle, cardiac muscle also works without your control. Cardiac muscle cells all contract together to make the heart beat.

Visual Connection
See Muscle Tissue in the student text, page 359.

Activity
Muscle Movement See student text, page 361.

 What are three different types of muscles in your body?

_____ _____ _____

How do skeletal muscles, tendons, and joints work together to make bones move?

A tendon is a tissue that connects skeletal muscle to bone. Tendons are very strong. When a muscle contracts, it pulls on a tendon. The tendon then pulls on a bone and makes it move.

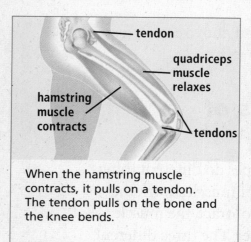

tendon

quadriceps muscle relaxes

hamstring muscle contracts

tendons

When the hamstring muscle contracts, it pulls on a tendon. The tendon pulls on the bone and the knee bends.

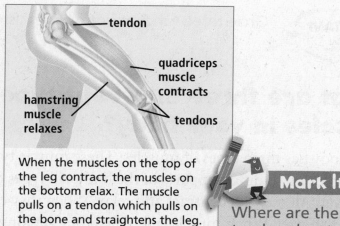

tendon

quadriceps muscle contracts

hamstring muscle relaxes

tendons

When the muscles on the top of the leg contract, the muscles on the bottom relax. The muscle pulls on a tendon which pulls on the bone and straightens the leg.

Mark It Up

Where are the tendons located in the drawings? Circle each tendon that is shown.

 What is a tendon? _____

_____

How do muscles change?

A newborn baby cannot do much with its muscles. A new baby cannot even lift its head or hold its head up. Over time, the baby's muscles develop and strengthen. The human muscular system develops through childhood and into adolescence. If you exercise every day, your muscles may get bigger. You do not actually get more muscles, but your muscles grow in size and strength.

Sometimes muscles can get damaged. A muscle can be stretched too much or even torn. The body then needs time to remove or repair the hurt cells. Over time, the muscle can heal.

 What happens if a muscle gets torn? _____

_____

SECTION 10.2

SUMMARIZE	VOCABULARY
1. How do muscles, tendons, and bones work together to make the body move? _____ _____ _____ _____ _____ _____ _____	**skeletal muscle smooth muscle** **cardiac muscle** **2.** What kind of muscle makes your heart beat? _____ **3.** What kind of muscle would you use to kick a soccer ball? _____ **4.** What kind of muscle helps you digest food and is not under your control? _____

Student text pages
364–369

How do muscles apply forces?

A **force** is energy that causes something to move. A force may cause a push or a pull. When you push or pull on a door, you are applying a force. The forces exerted* by your body come from your muscles. Forces can change the motion of an object. When you pick up a bag, throw a ball, or write with a pencil you are changing the motion of objects around you.

Activity

Force and Motion
See student text, page 364.

Size of a Force

The effect of a force depends on the size of the force. If you push on a door, and the door is stuck, you have to push harder. You need to use more force. A bigger force has a bigger effect. The effect of a force also depends on the direction of the force. A force is most effective when muscles pull in the direction in which the joints move most easily.

Balancing Forces

Weight is the downward force due to gravity. Weight is a force that is always acting on the body. Try holding your arm out straight in front of you. After a while it gets tired. When you hold your arm out, you are applying a force against gravity. Even though your arm is not moving, you are still applying a force.

When forces are balanced, there is no motion. Imagine what happens when two teams pull on opposite sides of a rope, as shown in the drawing below. If both sides pull with the same force, the rope stays in the same place. The rope will move only if one team pulls with more force than the other team.

balanced forces

*Academic Vocabulary: **Exert** means to use or apply a force. You **exert** a lot of force when you lift a heavy box from the floor.

Which body parts function like simple machines?

A **simple machine** is one of six tools—a pulley, lever, screw, wheel and axle, wedge, or inclined plane. These tools make some tasks easier. When a task is easy, you need less force to do it. Two or more simple machines may be used together to make other machines.

Activity

Changing Force
See student text, page 367.

We can compare the way joints in your body work to the way some simple machines work. The three simple machines that have similar movements in the body are pulleys, inclined planes, and levers.

What are three simple machines that work in the same way as some joints in the body?

_____ _____ _____

Pulleys

Pulleys let you change the direction of a force. For example, a pulley allows you to use the downward pull of your weight to lift a heavy object up. Your muscles, tendons, and joints sometimes work together in the same way as a pulley. They let you change the direction of a force.

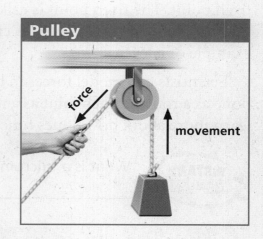

Pulley

force

movement

Muscles that are attached to two bones work like pulleys. The muscles are attached to one bone, stretched across a joint, and are attached to another bone. The joint can act like a pulley. It changes the direction that the force is applied. Hold out your arm so that it is straight. When you move your hand toward your shoulder, your bicep on top of your arm contracts. Although your hand is moving up, your muscle is pulling in a different direction. This movement is like a pulley. Your shoulders and wrists are also examples of joints that can act as pulleys.

What is one joint that can act like a pulley?

_____

Inclined Planes

An inclined plane, or a ramp, can help move a heavy object. Instead of lifting a heavy box, you can push it up a ramp. This moves the box higher, but it takes less force than lifting. Gliding joints, found in the wrists and feet, have slightly slanted surfaces that can function like inclined planes. These joints let your feet adjust to changes in the ground as you walk. And they use less force than if your ankle had to lift your body weight each time you stepped on uneven ground.

Inclined Plane

force

movement

 Which joints in the body have slanted surfaces, like inclined planes? _____

Levers

A lever is a solid bar, or rod, that moves around a fixed point. The fixed point is called a fulcrum. The fulcrum in the picture is blue. A crowbar is one example of a lever.

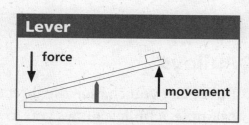

Lever

force

movement

Scientists can model forces in body movements by thinking of each bone as a rod and each joint as a fulcrum. In the next section, you will learn more about how bones function as levers.

 What is a fulcrum? _____
_____

SECTION 10.3	
SUMMARIZE	**VOCABULARY**
1. What are three simple machines that can model movement in the body? _____ _____ _____	Fill in the blanks with the correct term. **force** **simple machine** **balanced forces** 2. Muscles apply _____ that produces motion. 3. Some joints function like _____. 4. _____ produce no motion.

How are your limbs like levers?

Activity

Changing Forces
See student text,
page 371.

Remember that a **lever** is a rod that turns around a fixed point. You can think of a bone as a rod and a joint as the fixed point. When you bend your arm, you are moving the forearm around the joint in your elbow. Your arm acts like a lever. Most of the time, several levers work together to move legs and arms. Your legs and arms have many levers, powered by muscles.

 Fill in the blanks. Your limbs are like levers. A bone

is the _____ that moves around a

_____, or fixed point.

How do levers change the effects of a force?

Levers can increase the effect of a force. The effect depends on how the lever is used.

Fulcrum

Recall that the **fulcrum** is the fixed point of a lever, around which the rod turns. The fulcrum can be anywhere along a lever. It can be in the middle, like a see-saw. It can be at one end, like on a stapler. Or, it can be anywhere in between. The farther from the fulcrum a force is applied, the more effectively the lever is turned.

Mark It Up

Circle the fulcrum of the stapler.

fulcrum

If you press a stapler at the end farthest from the fulcrum it works best.

 Why is it most effective to push the free end of a stapler, not the middle? Use the word *fulcrum* in your response.

_____

_____

Input Force and Output Force

Input force is the force applied to a machine such as a lever. When you press on one end of a lever, you are applying an input force. The **output force** is the force that the machine exerts on an object. The input force on a body limb comes from muscles pulling on bone. When you flex your biceps, it exerts an input force on the lever of the forearm.

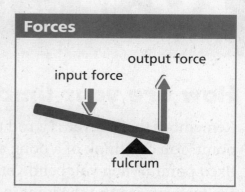

Forces

input force → output force
fulcrum

A lever can change a small input force into a large output force. For example, you might not be able to lift a large rock. But if you use a shovel, you can probably lift it. You use a small input force, and it produces a large output force.

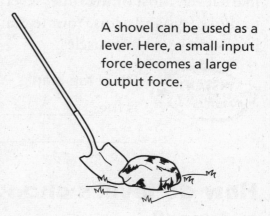

A shovel can be used as a lever. Here, a small input force becomes a large output force.

Other levers, including many of the levers found in the body, change a big input force into a small output force. However, you gain a bigger range of motion. A big force that moves a small distance lets your muscles move parts of your body over a bigger distance.

Many levers in the body change a big input force into a smaller output force. What is one benefit of this arrangement?_____

_____

How do different lever arrangements affect mechanical advantage?

The lever formed by your arm has a different arrangement than the lever formed by the shovel in the drawing above. One important difference between these two levers is in mechanical advantage. **Mechanical advantage** is a number that describes how much force comes out of a machine compared with how much force goes into it.

CLASSZONE.COM

Simulation Explore how a lever works.

What is mechanical advantage? Underline the sentence that tells you.

We can compare the mechanical advantage of different levers. If the input and output forces of a lever are equal, then the mechanical advantage is 1. If a small input force results in a bigger output force—such as with the shovel and rock—then the mechanical advantage is greater than 1.

If a big input force results in a smaller output force, the mechanical advantage is less than 1. Many levers in your body have a mechanical advantage less than 1. Instead of mechanical advantage, the body has speed and a big range of motion.

Under what conditions does a lever have a mechanical advantage that is less than 1? _____
_____

Classes of Levers

The fulcrum of a lever can be found anywhere along the rod. The input and output forces can also be found at different places on a lever. Levers are grouped into three different types. The three types of levers have different arrangements of the output force, input force, and fulcrum.

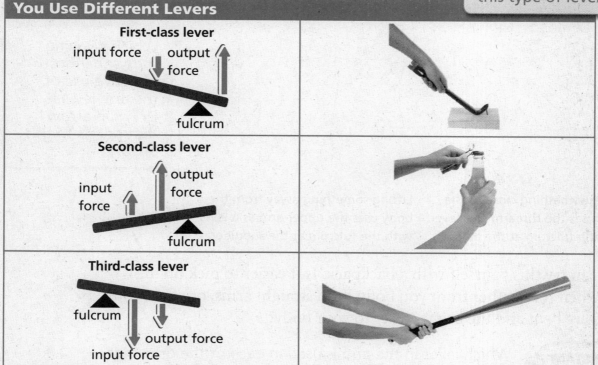

You Use Different Levers

First-class lever
input force   output force
fulcrum

Second-class lever
input force   output force
fulcrum

Third-class lever
fulcrum
output force
input force

What are the names of the three types of levers?

_____ _____ _____

How can you use your body's levers most effectively?

Your body is full of bones and joints that act like levers. Many of the bones and joints in your arms, legs, hands, and feet act like levers. Your hips, shoulders, and back also act like levers.

When you use a lever, it puts stress on the lever and the fulcrum. In your body, this means that it puts stress on the bone and the joint. You can use your knowledge of levers to limit the stress on your bones and joints and to protect your body. For example, if you bend over to lift something, it turns your back into a lever. This puts stress on your spine. If you bend your knees and use your legs to lift something, you use your leg bones as levers. The strong muscles in your thighs and calves then provide the input force.

You can also use your knowledge to make tasks easier or more effective. When you lift something close to your body, you use the levers in your arms more effectively than when you lift something farther away from your body.

Lifting something close to the body uses the forearm as a lever with the fulcrum at the elbow.

Lifting something away from the body uses the upper arm as a lever with the fulcrum at the shoulder.

Mark It Up

Which drawing shows the most effective use of the arm levers? Draw an arrow that points to this picture.

You can try this yourself with a backpack. Is it easier to pick up the bag when it is farther from you body, with straight arms, or when your arms are bent and the bag is closer to your body?

Which lever in the arm is used in each of the drawings above? Left drawing: _____

Right drawing: _____

Your hand and arm can act like a lever in different ways, depending on the motions you make. Your hand is a lever with the fulcrum at the wrist. Your forearm is a lever with a fulcrum at the elbow. Your upper arm is a lever with a fulcrum at the shoulder. You can use your body to combine the effects of different levers.

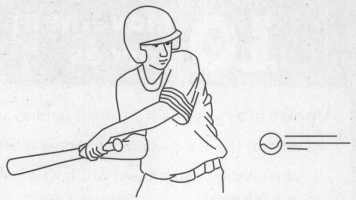

Athletes try to get the best combination of power and speed, using their entire bodies.

 What are three different parts of your arm that can act like a lever?

_____   _____   _____

SECTION 10.4	
SUMMARIZE	**VOCABULARY**
1. What is one example of a lever in your body? Identify the fulcrum of the lever. _____ _____ _____ _____	Circle the correct term to complete each sentence. 2. A bone acts as a lever with a joint as its **input force / fulcrum.** 3. The output force compared to input force is the **mechanical advantage / fulcrum** of a lever.

🌐 CLASSZONE.COM
Go to ClassZone.com
for activities, links, and
more test practice.

Vocabulary Circle the correct term to answer each question.

1 What is the place where two bones meet—a **joint** or a **lever?**

2 What is the point around which a lever moves—an **input force** or a **fulcrum?**

Reviewing Key Concepts

3 Describe the main functions of the skeletal system. _____
_____

4 Give a brief description of each type of muscle. Include whether or not it functions with your control or without your control:

_____

_____

_____

the BIG idea

5 When a shovel is used to pry up a rock, it uses a small input force and produces a large output force. Compare this type of lever to the levers in your body. Mention the trade-off between mechanical advantage and range of motion.

_____

_____

_____

_____

Test Practice

6 A force is a

   A lever
   B push or a pull
   C mechanical advantage
   D simple machine

7 Which two body systems function together to allow for movement?

   A endocrine and nervous systems
   B skeletal and endocrine systems
   C muscular and digestive systems
   D muscular and skeletal systems

11 Fluids, Pressure, and Circulation

the BIG idea

The body uses fluid pressure in many ways.

Getting Ready to Learn

Review Concepts

- Cells make up tissues, which make up organs, which make up organ systems.
- The circulatory system transports materials.
- Organ systems work together.

Activity

Heart Pumping
See student text, page 385.

Review Vocabulary

Draw a line to connect each word to its definition.

1. **tissue**
2. **organ**
3. **force**

a. push or a pull
b. group of similar cells
c. group of tissues

Preview Key Vocabulary

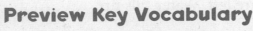

Use the frames to write important details about each of the terms.

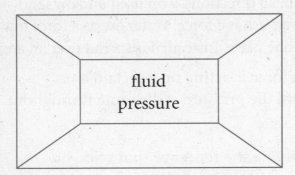

fluid pressure

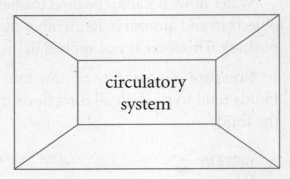

circulatory system

Student text pages 387–391

What is a fluid?

A **fluid** is a material that can flow easily, such as a gas or a liquid. Liquid water is a fluid. Air and other gases are fluids. Fluids flow to fit the shape of their containers.

Fluids are important to living things. Organisms use fluids such as water and air to survive. Much of the cytoplasm of a cell is made of fluids. Your body uses many fluids, such as blood.

 Circle all of the following materials that are fluids: ice, air, wood, water, blood

Fluids fill the shape of their containers.

How do fluids exert pressure?

Think about what happens when you pour water into a glass. No matter what the shape of the glass, the water will flow and fill the space of the glass. No empty holes are left. Water fills up spaces in any direction it can move.

Water flows because the fluid pushes in all directions—on itself and on solid objects in and around it. Remember that a push is a force. Water exerts a force by pushing. This force is not applied in just one place. Instead, it is spread over an area.

Pressure is a measure of how much force is acting on a certain area. Fluids tend to push in all directions until the pressure is the same throughout the fluid.

 What is pressure? Underline the sentence that tells you.

Breathing

When you breathe, air moves from areas of higher pressure to lower pressure. Your body is surrounded by air on the outside. This outside air presses against your body. The air inside your lungs presses outward. You make air move by changing the pressure of air in your lungs.

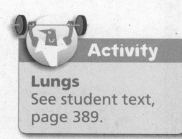

Activity

Lungs
See student text, page 389.

Inhaling Look at the picture. To breathe in, muscles in and below the rib cage pull downward and outward on your lungs. Your lungs are slightly elastic, like a balloon. When your lungs stretch, they can hold more air. The air inside expands to fill the larger space. This makes the air pressure inside the lungs lower. The air outside is at a higher pressure. The air outside your body moves into your lungs until the pressures are equal both inside and outside your body.

Exhaling To breathe out, muscles squeeze the lungs in and up. This compresses* the air in your lungs. The air in your lungs is now at a higher pressure than the air around you. Air rushes out through your open mouth until the pressures inside and outside your lungs are the same.

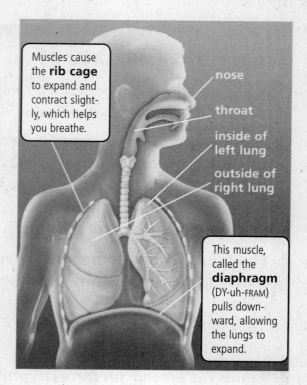

Muscles cause the **rib cage** to expand and contract slightly, which helps you breathe.

nose

throat

inside of left lung

outside of right lung

This muscle, called the **diaphragm** (DY-uh-FRAM) pulls downward, allowing the lungs to expand.

 **INSTANT REPLAY** When the air pressure inside your lungs is lower than the air pressure outside your body, do you breathe in or out? _____

How is pressure related to force and area?

If a lot of force is applied over a small area, there is great pressure. If the same amount of force is applied over a larger area, there would be less pressure. Pressure describes how concentrated a force is. The more force, the more pressure. The smaller the area over which a force is applied, the more pressure.

 **INSTANT REPLAY** Circle the sentence that describes the most pressure:
A large force applied over a small area.
A large force applied over a large area.

*Academic Vocabulary: To **compress** means to push in or make more compact. You might sit on top of a suitcase to **compress** the clothes inside so that you can zip the suitcase shut.

What are three main ways your body uses fluid pressure?

Fluids in your body can be gases, liquids, and even mixtures of gases, liquids, and solids. Your body uses fluid pressure in three main ways:

1. **Fluids in your body can transfer forces.** Do you remember ever getting a shot at the doctor's office? Getting a shot through a syringe is an example of fluids transfering forces. When the doctor pushes on the end of the syringe, it puts pressure on the liquid. The liquid transfers the force from the end of the syringe to the tip of the syringe.

2. **Fluids in your body can move materials around.** Pressure also moves a fluid. Think again about the syringe. The pressure at the open tip of the syringe is lower than the liquid pressure inside. The liquid moves toward this area of lower pressure and squirts out of the syringe.

3. **Fluids can spread out forces to protect your body.** If you squeeze one end of a full balloon, it probably won't pop. This is because when you squeeze it, the air spreads out the force to the whole balloon.

Pushing on the end of the syringe forces the fluid out.

 Underline the three main ways your body uses fluids.

SECTION 11.1

SUMMARIZE	VOCABULARY
1. Compare the pressure of air inside your lungs and outside your body by completing these sentences: When you breathe in _____ _____ When you breathe out _____ _____	Circle the term or terms that completes each sentence. 2. **Pressure / concentration** is a measure of how much force is acting on a certain area. 3. Air and water are examples of **forces / fluids.** 4. Fluids move from an area of **higher / lower** pressure to an area of **higher / lower** pressure.

Student text pages
393–399

What is the circulatory system?

Blood moves around the body in the circulatory system, which includes the heart and blood vessels. You can think of the circulatory system as a container that holds blood.

Activity

Blood Pressure
See student text,
page 393.

Blood is a fluid. It contains some solids, including red and white blood cells and small pieces of cells. These solid pieces are carried in a liquid called plasma. The plasma is made of water, proteins, sugars, and other materials. Together, the liquid and solid parts act as a fluid.

How does blood pressure affect the circulatory system?

Blood moves throughout your body in blood vessels. Blood vessels are flexible and tube-shaped. They have different diameters, some large and some small.

The diameter of a tube is the distance across the opening

- An **artery** is a blood vessel that carries blood away from the heart, toward another part of the body.

- A **vein** is a vessel that carries blood toward the heart.

 **INSTANT REPLAY** What is the difference between an artery and a vein?

_____

Differences in pressure make blood move. Each time the heart beats, it pushes blood into large arteries. The pressure is high, so the blood moves toward areas of lower pressure. In this way, blood pressure keeps blood moving in the body.

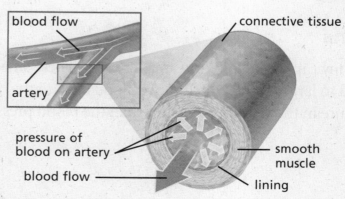

blood flow

artery

connective tissue

pressure of blood on artery

blood flow

smooth muscle

lining

When the heart beats, it causes blood pressure.

Arteries

Blood pushes outward on the blood vessel as it flows. The blood leaving the heart is at high pressure, so arteries must have thick, strong walls.

Large arteries branch into smaller and smaller arteries. Blood spreads out as it moves into the many smaller vessels. This results in lower pressure on the walls of the smaller vessels. Smaller blood vessels have thinner walls than larger vessels. Blood flows through smaller and smaller arteries into the capillaries.

 Where is blood pressure greater—close to the heart or far from the heart?

_____

Capillaries

Capillaries are the smallest blood vessels. They bring blood close to every cell in the body. The walls of capillaries are very thin. They are made of just one layer of cells. Blood plasma and other materials move through the capillary walls toward other body cells. Fluids and waste materials move from body cells into the capillaries and become part of the blood.

 Which blood vessels are smallest—arteries, capillaries, or veins? _____

Veins

The tiny capillaries join into smaller veins. These smaller veins carry the blood to larger veins, which move blood back to the heart. The blood pressure in the veins is much less than the blood pressure in the arteries.

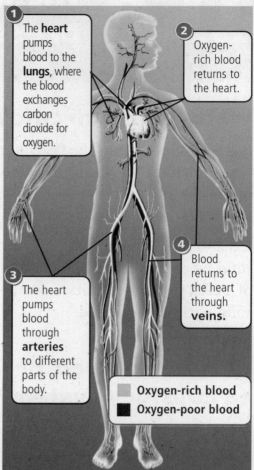

1. The **heart** pumps blood to the **lungs**, where the blood exchanges carbon dioxide for oxygen.

2. Oxygen-rich blood returns to the heart.

3. The heart pumps blood through **arteries** to different parts of the body.

4. Blood returns to the heart through **veins**.

■ Oxygen-rich blood
■ Oxygen-poor blood

How does blood move through the heart?

The heart supplies the pressure to move blood through the circulatory system. You can think of the heart as two pumps. A pump is something that moves fluids. Each side of the heart is a pump.

- The right side of the heart pumps blood to the lungs.

- The left side then pumps the blood to the rest of the body

Each side of the heart is made up of an upper and a lower part.

- The upper part of each side is called an atrium (AY-tree-uhm). The atrium collects blood for pumping.

- The lower part of each side is called a ventricle. The ventricle pumps blood out of the heart.

Vocabulary

Reading Tip
The plural of *atrium* is *atria.*

The lower part—the ventricle—of the left side of the heart is the strongest. This is the part of the heart that pumps blood through the whole body. Use the diagram below to follow the path of blood.

Note that when we talk about the right and left sides of your heart, it is from your own point of view. The left side of your heart is the side nearest your left arm. The right side of your heart is nearest your right arm. If you turn the book around so the diagram below faces out and hold it against your chest, the drawing will show the heart as it looks in the body.

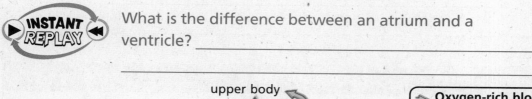

INSTANT REPLAY What is the difference between an atrium and a ventricle? _____

_____

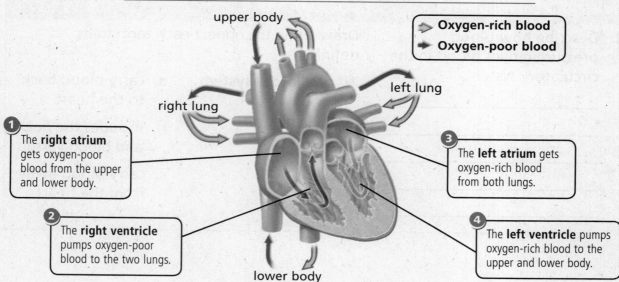

upper body

Oxygen-rich blood
Oxygen-poor blood

left lung

right lung

1. The **right atrium** gets oxygen-poor blood from the upper and lower body.

3. The **left atrium** gets oxygen-rich blood from both lungs.

2. The **right ventricle** pumps oxygen-poor blood to the two lungs.

4. The **left ventricle** pumps oxygen-rich blood to the upper and lower body.

lower body

Heart Valves

The first part of your heartbeat is the contraction of the atria. This pushes blood into the ventricles. Valves prevent blood from moving back into the atria from the ventricles.

A valve is a structure that opens and closes. Heart valves are one-way. Blood can pass through heart valves in one direction only. The blood cannot move backwards. The drawings below show how the valves open and close as the heart beats.

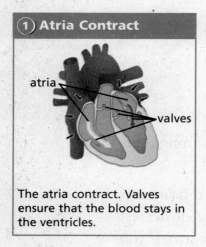

① Atria Contract

atria

valves

The atria contract. Valves ensure that the blood stays in the ventricles.

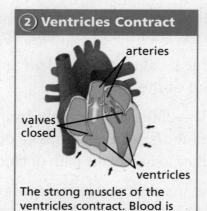

② Ventricles Contract

arteries

valves closed

ventricles

The strong muscles of the ventricles contract. Blood is pushed out of the heart.

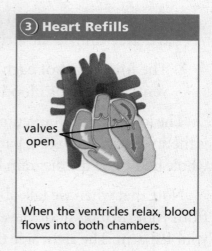

③ Heart Refills

valves open

When the ventricles relax, blood flows into both chambers.

INSTANT REPLAY

What is the function of heart valves?

_____

SECTION 11.2

SUMMARIZE

1. Describe how blood pressure moves blood in the circulatory system.

_____

_____

_____

_____

_____

VOCABULARY

Draw a line to connect each term to its definition.

2. **circulatory system**

3. **arteries**

4. **veins**

a. carry blood back to the heart

b. includes the heart and blood vessels

c. carry blood away from the heart

Student text pages
402–408

What are some of the functions of fluids in the body?

Fluids serve many functions in the body. Your body uses blood to transport materials. Tears are a fluid that helps to protect your eyes and wash out particles. Tears also help your eyelids move smoothly and keep the eye surface from drying out.

Visual Connection
See Functions of Fluids in the student text, page 403.

Mucus is a fluid that forms a protective coating in several parts of your body. Cells in your nose, throat, and other places produce mucus. Mucus has many jobs. It protects tissue from drying out. It blocks materials from reaching the tissue under the mucus. It also helps move some materials. Other fluids play other roles in the body.

List at least two functions of fluids in the body.

_____

What roles do fluids have in your eyes and ears?

Activity

Semicircular Canals
See student text, page 405.

Fluids play important roles in your ears and eyes.

The Ear Fluid inside tiny spaces in your ears helps you sense your balance, position, and motion. The **semicircular canals** are three tiny spaces where fluids help you sense the motion of your head. They help you feel your head nodding up and down, turning side-to-side, and tilting to one side or the other. You will learn more about sound and hearing in Chapter 12.

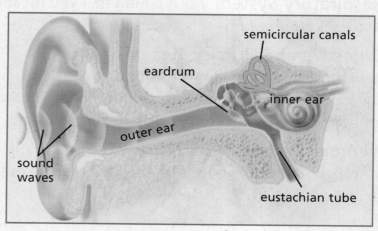

semicircular canals

eardrum

inner ear

outer ear

sound waves

eustachian tube

The Eye Tears help wash particles away from your eyes and help your eyelids move smoothly. Fluids also work inside the eye.

Look at the diagram on the right. The clear front of the eye is called the cornea. Behind the cornea is a space filled with a clear gel fluid. This fluid carries nutrients to the eye's lens and cornea. It also carries away waste material. You will learn more about eyes and vision in Chapter 14.

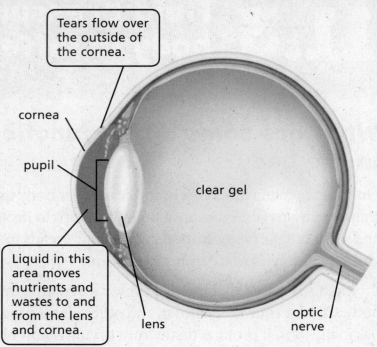

Tears flow over the outside of the cornea.

cornea

pupil

clear gel

Liquid in this area moves nutrients and wastes to and from the lens and cornea.

lens

optic nerve

What is the cornea?

_____

How do the body's organ systems use fluids?

You have read about fluids in the circulatory system, respiratory system, ears, and eyes. In fact, all of your organ systems use fluids.

Circulatory System Blood and plasma are fluids in your circulatory system.

Respiratory System Air is a fluid that you breathe in and out. Mucus is also made by this system.

Digestive and Urinary Systems Your stomach contains fluids that help move and break down the food you eat. In your urinary system, the kidneys remove wastes from your blood. The wastes and a small amount of water exit your body as urine each day.

Nervous System Fluids help protect your brain and spinal cord. If you shake or bump your head, the fluids spread out the force, so less damage is done to the tissues.

Muscular and Skeletal Systems Your muscular system needs large supplies of nutrients and makes large amounts of wastes. Both nutrients and wastes are transported by blood. Your skeletal system uses fluids, too. For example, fluids help your joints move easily.

 Name at least three fluids that are important for your body's organ systems.

_____

Reproductive System The female and male reproductive systems use fluids. For example, a fetus develops inside a fluid-filled sac. The fluid gives support and protection to the fetus. Fluids in the male and female reproductive systems can also transport diseases. Sexually transmitted diseases such as HIV, genital herpes, gonorrhea, and syphilis are passed from one person to another through the fluids of the reproductive system.

 What is one disease that can be transported from person to person in reproductive fluids?

_____

SECTION 11.3	
SUMMARIZE	**VOCABULARY**
1. Describe at least one role of fluids in the eyes and ears. Ears: _____ _____ Eyes: _____ _____ _____	Fill in the blanks with the term that makes the sentences correct. **semicircular canals respiratory mucus** 2. _____ is a fluid made by the _____ system. 3. The _____ are found in the ears and help you sense different motions.

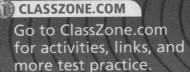

CLASSZONE.COM
Go to ClassZone.com for activities, links, and more test practice.

Vocabulary Fill in each blank with the correct word from the list.

| fluid |
| pressure |
| mucus |

1 Air and blood are two _____ that your body uses.

2 _____ is a measurement of how much force is acting on a certain area.

Reviewing Key Concepts

3 Describe how air pressure inside your lungs changes as you breathe. _____
_____
_____
_____

4 Semicircular canals are located in your ears. Describe the role of this structure and of the fluids it contains. _____
_____
_____

the BIG idea

5 Give at least two examples of how fluids are used in the body's systems. _____
_____

Test Practice

6 Which structures help prevent blood from flowing backwards in the heart?

  A valves
  B mucus
  C veins
  D semicircular canals

7 What is the cornea?

  A the small bone in the ear
  B the surface of the eye
  C the valve in the heart
  D the vein in the artery

12 Sound

The ear responds to sound waves.

Getting Ready to Learn

Review Concepts

- Energy can be transferred from one place to another.
- Forces can cause changes in motion.

Activity

How Does a Sound Change If You Move Your Head? See student text, page 421.

Review Vocabulary

Draw a line to connect each term with its definition.

fluid   chamber in the inner ear that senses movement and balance

semicircular canals   substance that can flow easily

Preview Key Vocabulary

As you read about each part of the ear, label the names of the structures marked on the drawing below. Under the name, write the function of each structure.

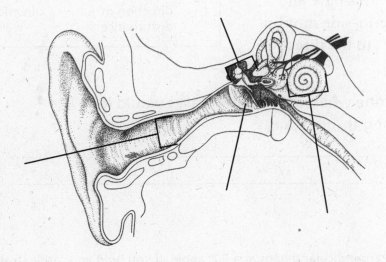

Student text pages
423–430

What is sound?

Vibrations are quick back-and-forth movements of matter. Vibrations cause sound. **Sound** is a wave that travels through matter. A **wave** is a disturbance that transfers energy from one place to another.

Activity

Sound
See student text, page 423.

How do sound waves move through air and other matter?

Sound waves travel through air, liquids, and solid materials. A substance that sound and other waves travel through is called a **medium.** Air is a medium made up of molecules of different gases.

We cannot see sound waves, but we can imagine what sound waves look like. Sound is a longitudinal wave. This means that the vibrations move in the same direction as the wave.

Transverse waves are a different kind of wave. Transverse waves have an up-and-down or side-to-side motion that is perpendicular* to the direction the wave travels.

CLASSZONE.COM

Simulation Explore how sound travels through air.

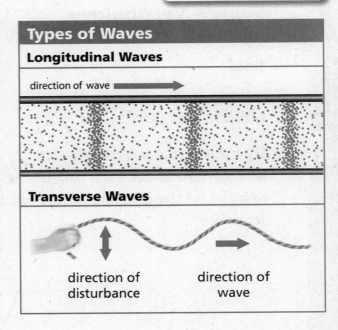

Types of Waves

Longitudinal Waves

direction of wave

Transverse Waves

direction of disturbance

direction of wave

Describe what longitudinal waves would look like moving through air.

_____

_____

*Academic Vocabulary: **Perpendicular** means at a 90° angle. If you hold your arms straight out in front of you at shoulder height, they will be **perpendicular** to your body.

How do different mediums affect the speed of sound waves?

Sound travels faster in water than in air. The molecules of water are packed closer together than the molecules of different gases in air. It takes less time for the water molecules to bump into one another. Sound moves even faster through solid materials. The temperature of the medium also affects the speed of sound.

Materials and Sound Speeds		
Medium	**State**	**Speed of Sound**
Air (20°C)	Gas	344 m/s (769 mi/h)
Water (20°C)	Liquid	1400 m/s (3130 mi/h)
Steel (20°C)	Solid	5000 m/s (11,200 mi/h)

Activity

Wave Types
See student text, page 426.

What are three properties of sound and other waves?

You've read about one property of waves—speed. Two other important properties of waves are frequency and wavelength. Moving waves have bumps and valleys. One bump and one valley is a cycle.

- **Frequency** is the number of cycles in a given amount of time. The unit for measuring frequency is the hertz. One **hertz** (Hz) is one cycle per second.

- **Wavelength** is the distance from any point of one cycle to the identical point of the next cycle.

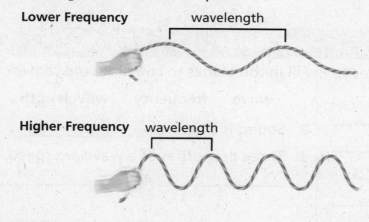

Lower Frequency   wavelength

Higher Frequency   wavelength

Fill in the blanks: Three properties of waves are

_____, _____,

and _____.

How are frequency, wavelength, and speed related?

The relationship between frequency, wavelength, and speed can be expressed in a formula.

$$\text{wavelength} = \frac{\text{speed}}{\text{frequency}}$$

Let's find the wavelength of the musical note middle C. We can use the speed and frequency to find the wavelength. The speed of sound in air is about 340 meters per second (m/s). The frequency of middle C is 256 hertz.

$$\text{wavelength} = \frac{340 \text{ m/s}}{256 \text{ Hz}} = 1.32 \text{ meters}$$

Different musical notes have different wavelengths and frequencies.

The wavelength of middle C is about 1.3 meters (4.4 ft). How long is the wavelength of middle C compared to your spread arms?

 **INSTANT REPLAY** How are frequency, wavelength, and speed related? Circle the formula that shows their relationship.

SECTION 12.1

SUMMARIZE	VOCABULARY
1. Use two or three sentences to explain what sound is.	Fill in the blanks to complete the sentences.
_____	**wave frequency wavelength**
_____	2. Sound is a type of _____.
_____	3. Three properties of a wave are speed,
_____	_____ and _____.
_____	

Student text pages 432–437

What makes a sound high or low?

The highness or lowness of a sound is called **pitch.** A whistle is a high-pitched sound. A tuba makes a lower-pitched sound. The pitch of a sound depends on the frequency of the sound wave.

Activity

Pitch
See student text, page 432.

The picture below shows a high-frequency and a low-frequency wave. An object vibrating very fast makes a high-pitched sound. The same object makes a lower-pitched sound when it vibrates more slowly.

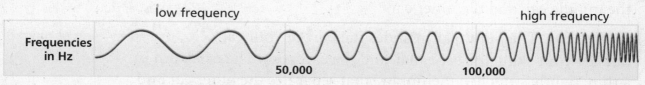

low frequency   high frequency

Frequencies in Hz   50,000   100,000

When you speak or sing, sound is produced by the vocal cords in your throat. You can make higher-pitched sounds when your vocal cords are tense. When they are less tense, you can produce lower-pitched sounds.

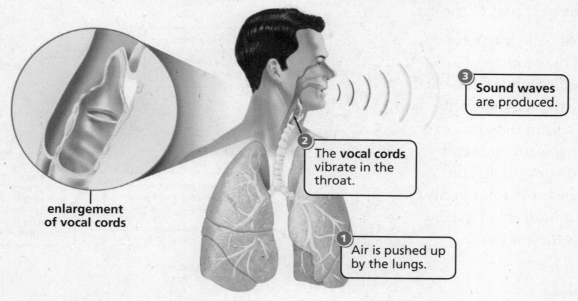

3 Sound waves are produced.

2 The **vocal cords** vibrate in the throat.

enlargement of vocal cords

1 Air is pushed up by the lungs.

INSTANT REPLAY

Underline the type of sound wave that has a higher frequency—**one that makes a high-pitched sound** or **one that makes a low-pitched sound.**

Which frequencies of sound can humans hear?

Hertz is a unit for measuring frequency. Some animals can hear only a very small range of sound frequencies. A mosquito, for example, can hear sounds only between 200–400 Hz. Other animals can hear a huge range of sounds. A porpoise, for example, can hear sounds between 75–150,000 Hz. Humans can hear sounds in the range of 20–20,000 Hz.

Visual Connection
Sound Frequencies Heard by Animals See student text, page 434.

What are the three main parts of the human ear?

The three main parts of the human ear are the outer ear, the middle ear, and the inner ear.

CLASSZONE.COM
Visualization See the process of hearing in action.

Outer Ear The **outer ear** includes the part of your ear outside your skull, the ear canal, and the eardrum. The **eardrum** is a thin, tightly stretched membrane that separates the outer ear and middle ear. Sound waves cause the eardrum to vibrate.

Middle Ear The **middle ear** is a space filled with air. It contains three tiny, connected bones. Vibrations move the bones. The movement affects the next part of the ear.

Inner Ear The **inner ear** contains the semicircular canals and another fluid-filled structure that is shaped like a snail. Cells in the inner ear sense movement and send signals to your brain. You actually hear the sound only after your brain receives and processes these signals.

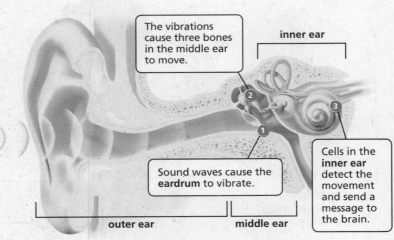

The vibrations cause three bones in the middle ear to move.

inner ear

Sound waves cause the **eardrum** to vibrate.

Cells in the **inner ear** detect the movement and send a message to the brain.

outer ear

middle ear

What do vibrations move in the middle ear?

_____

Have you ever listened to a recording of your voice? If so, you may have noticed that the recording sounds different from the way your voice sounds to you when you speak normally.

When you listen to the recording, the sound waves are traveling to you through the air. When you speak normally, the vibrations travel through the air—but they also travel through your body to your eardrums. The vibrations in your body are at different frequencies than the vibrations in the air.

INSTANT REPLAY Why does a recording of your voice sound different to you than when you talk? _____
_____
_____
_____

SECTION 12.2

SUMMARIZE	VOCABULARY
1. Describe the movement of sound waves through the three main parts of your ear. **Outer Ear:** _____ _____ _____ **Middle Ear:** _____ _____ _____ **Inner Ear:** _____ _____ _____	Draw a line to connect each word to its definition. 2. vibration a. highness or lowness of a sound 3. eardrum b. back-and-forth movement of an object 4. pitch c. thin membrane in outer ear

Student text pages
440–444

How do structures in the inner ear respond to sound?

Recall that sound waves move through your ear canal to your eardrum. The sound waves cause the eardrum to vibrate. The vibrations move through the middle ear to the inner ear.

Activity

Frequency
See student text, page 441.

Inside the inner ear is the cochlea (KAWK-lee-uh). The cochlea is a small, curled structure that looks like a snail. The curled spaces are filled with fluid. When sound waves reach the inner ear, they cause changes in pressure, which causes the fluids to move. The moving fluid also affects tiny hair cells along the cochlea. When these hair cells move, they send electrical signals to the brain.

In which part of the ear is the cochlea found—the outer ear, middle ear, or inner ear? _____

How does loudness affect the ear?

What makes a whisper so soft and a shout so loud? Loudness depends on how compressed a sound wave is. Look at the picture. If a sound wave is more compressed, it hits your ear with a greater force and sounds louder. A less compressed sound wave sounds softer.

The loudness of a sound is described using a unit called a **decibel (dB).** A sound that is less than 10 decibels can barely be heard. A sound greater than 100 decibels is very loud and can hurt your ears.

less compressed =
softer sound

more compressed =
louder sound

A decibel is the measure of how loud or soft a sound is.

Your ears respond to loud noises in a way that reduces the effects of the sound. Two small muscles in the middle ear cause changes that result in less energy reaching the cochlea.

Loudness of Sounds

20 dB light rainfall

150 dB airplane taking off nearby

90 dB lawn mower

10 dB leaves rustling in the breeze

60 dB dog barking

These muscles help protect the ear, but very loud noises can still cause damage. An extremely loud noise can destroy the tiny hair cells in your cochlea. Loud sounds from noisy tools, noisy environments, headsets, earbuds, and rock concerts can all damage your ears.

One way to protect your ears from such loud noises is to use earplugs. Earplugs help to absorb some of the energy of the sound waves before it gets to the eardrum.

How do extremely loud noises affect the hair cells in the cochlea? _____

SECTION 12.3

SUMMARIZE	VOCABULARY
1. What is one structure in your inner ear that can be damaged by very loud sounds? _____ _____ _____ _____	Fill in the blanks to complete the sentences. **decibel cochlea** 2. Tiny hair cells in the _____ send signals to the brain. 3. The loudness of a sound is measured in _____.

Vocabulary Circle the phrase that answers each question.

1 Where is the eardrum located—in the **outer ear** or the **inner ear?**

2 What unit is used to measure loudness—the **hertz** or the **decibel?**

3 Where is the cochlea located—in the **middle ear** or the **inner ear?**

4 What is sound—a type of **wave** or **medium?**

Reviewing Key Concepts

5 Look at the drawings to the right. Circle the
   one that represents sound waves.

6 What is sound? _____
   _____

7 Name the three main sections of your ear.

   _____ _____

   _____

8 What are three structures found in your middle ear?

   _____

the BIG idea

9 Where are hair cells found, and how do they help you to hear?
   _____

Test Practice

10 Before you hear a sound, a sound
    wave must enter your ear and hit
    the

    A semicircular canals
    B eardrum
    C longitudinal vibrations
    D low decibels

11 Your ear has two structures that
    can reduce the loudness of a sound.
    What are these structures?

    A bones
    B outer ears
    C muscles
    D pitches

CHAPTER
13 Light

the **BIG** idea

Visible light is a small band of the electro-magnetic spectrum.

Getting Ready to Learn

Review Concepts

- A wave is a disturbance that transfers energy.
- Sound waves move through a medium.
- Frequency, wavelength, and speed are related.
- Waves react to change in a medium.

Activity

Seeing Color
See student text, page 451.

Review Vocabulary
Fill in the blanks with the correct term.

medium   **frequency**   **wavelength**

Two properties of waves are _____ and
_____.

Waves travel through a substance known as a _____.

Preview Key Vocabulary
Here are some terms you will learn in this chapter. As you read the chapter, write a sentence to explain how the terms are related. Write your sentences below.

Light _____ electromagnetic wave.

A rod cell _____ retina.

To absorb _____ to emit.

Student text pages 453–461

What is an electromagnetic wave?

An **electromagnetic wave** (ih-LEHK-troh-mag-NEHT-ihk) is a disturbance* in a field. A field is an area of space that can exert a force. Electromagnetic waves are also called EM waves. Visible light is one type of EM wave. Radio waves, microwaves, and X-rays are also EM waves. Most EM waves are invisible to humans.

CLASSZONE.COM

Visualization Learn more about the nature of EM waves.

Activity

Light
See student text, page 453.

What type of wave is visible light?

_____

Like sound and other waves, an EM wave has three important characteristics: speed, wavelength, and frequency. But EM waves move differently than do sound waves. EM waves tend to radiate, or spread out, from a source.

Waves and Particles

Scientists think of light in two different ways—as rays and as particles. Sometimes, scientists think of light as being made of many narrow rays, or beams, as shown in the drawing. You will use this ray model when you learn about lenses and images.

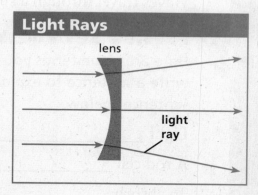

Light Rays

lens

light ray

Scientists also think about light as being made of tiny particles of energy. Matter **absorbs,** or takes in, light when it takes up a particle's energy.

What are two different ways that scientists think about light?

_____   _____

*Academic Vocabulary: **Disturbance** means a disruption or a change. If you have a fire drill at school, the drill might **disturb** your class time.

The Electromagnetic Spectrum

There are many different types of electromagnetic (EM) waves. The whole range of these EM waves makes up the **electromagnetic spectrum.** A spectrum (SPEHK-truhm) is a continuous range of something. For example, a rainbow is a spectrum of visible light.

Visual Connection
See The Electromagnetic Spectrum in the student text, pages 456–457.

What are the parts of the EM spectrum?

The EM spectrum includes many frequencies—from low frequencies to high frequencies. The different types of EM waves include radio waves, microwaves, infrared light, visible light, ultraviolet light, X-rays, and gamma rays. EM waves of different frequencies interact with matter in different ways.

The Sun produces all the different types of EM waves. People have also developed technologies that use and produce different EM waves. The different kinds of EM waves are shown in the graphic below.

What are some of the different types of EM waves? Underline the sentence that tells you.

The Electromagnetic Spectrum

Frequency in Hertz (1 Hz = 1 cycle/second)

10^4 10^5 10^6 10^7 10^8 10^9 10^{10} 10^{11} 10^{12} 10^{13} 10^{14} 10^{15} 10^{16} 10^{17} 10^{18} 10^{19} 10^{20} 10^{21} 10^{22} 10^{23} 10^{24}

Radio Waves Infrared Light Ultraviolet Light Gamma Rays

Microwaves visible light X-Rays

red violet

Radio Waves Radio waves are low-frequency waves. They are used to send radio and television signals.

Infrared Radiation (IR) You cannot see IR but you can feel it as it warms your skin.

Ultraviolet Light UV is invisible to humans, but it can cause damage to your skin. Some animals, such as bees, can see UV light.

Gamma Rays This is the highest-frequency range of the EM spectrum.

Microwaves Cell phones and microwave ovens are two technologies that use microwaves.

Visible Light The part of the EM spectrum that human eyes can see is called visible light. This is a small range of wavelengths in the spectrum.

X-Rays X-rays can pass through skin, muscle, and other soft tissues of the body. Too many X-rays can damage your body.

Visible Light

Visible light is a small part of the whole EM spectrum. Plants use this part of the EM spectrum for photosynthesis. Your ability to see depends on visible light.

Humans can see many frequencies of visible light. You see the lowest frequencies (longest wavelengths) as red. The highest frequencies (shortest wavelengths) look violet. You may have noticed that two other groups of EM waves are named for these colors: infrared and ultraviolet. Infrared waves have a frequency just lower than red. Ultraviolet waves have frequencies just higher than violet. These two frequencies are invisible to the naked eye.

Activity

Ultraviolet Light
See student text, page 460.

Which is a higher frequency of light—red or violet?

_____

SECTION 13.1

SUMMARIZE	VOCABULARY
1. How big is the range of visible light compared with the whole EM spectrum? _____ _____ _____ _____ _____	Fill in the blanks to complete the sentences. **electromagnetic spectrum** **visible light** 2. _____ is the part of the EM spectrum that humans can see. 3. Microwaves and X-rays are two different ranges of the _____ .

SECTION 13.2 — Light is produced in different ways.

Key Concept

Student text pages 463–467

How does light help you see?

When you go outside, you might see buildings, trees, and people. Light bounces off the objects and enters your eyes. Cells in your eyes absorb the light and send signals to your brain. Only then can you see the objects around you. But light does not need to bounce off some objects for you to see them. Some objects make their own light.

Glowing Objects

Some objects glow because they **emit,** or give off, visible light. Objects emit light by changing one form of energy into EM radiation. You see a glowing object when the light enters your eye and is absorbed.

What does the word *emit* mean? _____

Hot Objects

Hot objects produce light when they change energy into EM radiation. The hotter a material is, the more energy it can give off. Very hot objects—hundreds of degrees Celsius—can produce visible light.

A red-hot stove and a light bulb give off visible light because they are very hot. Light bulbs work by heating a thin wire with an electric current. As the thin wire gets hotter, it gives off visible light.

Hot matter can give off many different EM frequencies. A red-hot stove and a light bulb give off infrared light (as heat) and visible light.

What are two examples of hot matter that give off visible light?

_____

_____

Activity

Artificial Lighting
See student text, page 465.

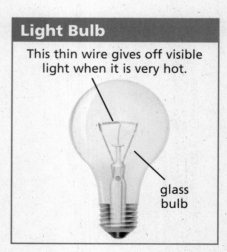

Light Bulb

This thin wire gives off visible light when it is very hot.

glass bulb

What are some other sources of energy that can produce light?

You just read that light can be produced from the energy of hot matter. Light can also be produced from other sources of energy. For example, some chemical reactions can produce light. Fireflies produce their own light with a chemical reaction.

Some lamps use charged particles to make gases glow. Neon gas, for example, can give off a lot of red light. Televisions also use charged particles to produce colored light.

This sign glows because its letters are filled with hot neon gas.

INSTANT REPLAY What are two sources of energy that can produce light?

_____ _____

SECTION 13.2	
SUMMARIZE	**VOCABULARY**
1. Match an example of each type of light to each energy source. a. hot matter televisions b. chemical reactions fireflies c. charged particles light bulbs	Circle the phrase that answers each question. 2. What does **emit** mean— to give off or to take in? 3. What gives off **visible light**— hot matter or cold matter?

SECTION
13.3

Key Concept
Light interacts with materials.

Student text pages
468–473

How does light interact with matter?

Light can interact with matter in three main ways. Visible light can pass through, bouce off, or be absorbed by different materials.

Transmit Matter can **transmit** light, or let it pass through. Some materials—such as air or clear glass—allow light to pass straight through. Other materials—such as clouds or thin paper—allow only some light to pass through. These materials **diffuse** (dih-FYOOZ) light, or cause it to spread out in many directions.

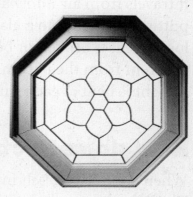

Windows allow light to pass through them. They transmit light.

What is one example of a material that diffuses light? _____

Reflect Visible light cannot pass through material, such as this book, that is not clear. These materials may **reflect** light, or cause light to bounce off them. Even some clear materials, such as water, can reflect light under the right conditions. However, these materials can also absorb light.

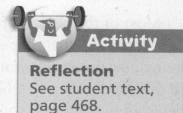

Activity

Reflection
See student text, page 468.

What does light do when it is reflected?

_____

Absorb Matter absorbs light by taking in the light's energy. Light can be absorbed at the surface of a material. For example, the ink on this page absorbs light. Light can also be absorbed as light travels through a material. For example, light is absorbed as it passes through lake water. The light travels below the water's surface. But most of the light is absorbed before reaching the lake's deep bottom.

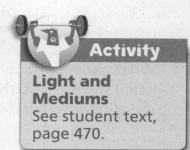

Activity

Light and Mediums
See student text, page 470.

Refraction

Light travels through a medium in a straight line. But light may change direction, or **refract,** if the medium that the light is traveling through changes. Light refracts when it changes speed. For example, light refracts when it travels from air into water or from water into air. Try putting a pencil into a glass of water. The pencil will look like it is broken or bent—the part underwater looks different from the part in the air. This is because the path of light is bent at each surface.

Refracted at a Surface

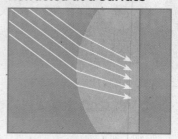

Light rays bend at the surface between two mediums—air and glass. Within a medium, the rays are straight.

How do reflections work?

When you see yourself in the mirror, you are seeing a regular reflection. The light rays come from one direction and all bounce off the mirror in the same direction. You may also be able to see your reflection in a glass window. Even though windows transmit most of the light that hits them, they also reflect some of the light.

Most of the objects around you reflect light in a different way. The light rays come from one direction, but they bounce off the surface in many new directions. Your skin and this page cause light to be reflected in this way. When light bounces off an object in this way and then is detected by your eye, you can see the object.

When you look in a mirror, in how many directions is light bouncing off of it? _____

SECTION 13.3	
SUMMARIZE	**VOCABULARY**
1. What happens to light when the medium that it is traveling through changes? _____ _____ _____ _____	Draw a line to connect each word to its description. 2. reflect a. pass through 3. refract b. bounce off 4. transmit c. take in 5. absorb d. change direction

13.4 Key Concept
Color comes from light.

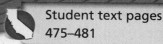

Student text pages
475–481

How do your eyes and brain help you see different colors?

Your eyes and brain work together in order for you to see. Here's how:

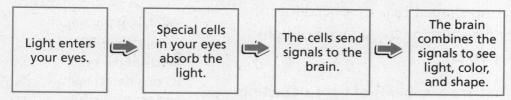

| Light enters your eyes. | ⇨ | Special cells in your eyes absorb the light. | ⇨ | The cells send signals to the brain. | ⇨ | The brain combines the signals to see light, color, and shape. |

Cells in your eyes respond to different frequencies of light. Different frequencies of light appear as different colors. If just one frequency of light enters your eyes, you see only one color. But most of the time objects emit or reflect many different frequencies at the same time.

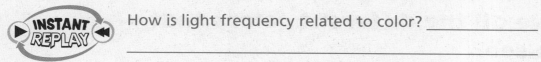

INSTANT REPLAY   How is light frequency related to color? _____

_____

Properties of Light

White light, such as sunlight, is a mixture of many different frequencies of light. You can use a prism to separate white light into a spectrum of different frequencies that looks like a rainbow.

Properties of the Eye

Your eyes detect* light by absorbing it. The more light that enters your eyes, the brighter an object looks. When your eyes absorb no light, an object looks very dark, and you cannot see it. When your eyes absorb a small amount of light, you see the object, but it still looks dark—unlit or black. When your eyes absorb more light, the object looks brighter.

*Academic Vocabulary: To **detect** means to sense something. You might **detect** that your dinner is burning when you smell smoke coming from the kitchen.

Cells inside your eyes absorb light. The **retina** (REHT-uhn-uh) is a layer of tissue inside each eye. Cells in the retina detect light and start signals that are sent to the brain. The retina has two types of light-detecting cells: rod cells and cone cells.

Rod cells are long, thin cells that let you see in dim light. Your rod cells simply tell your brain how bright the light is. They don't detectr color frequencies.

Cone cells are cone-shaped cells that need lots of light to work. They detect many frequencies of light and allow you to see color.

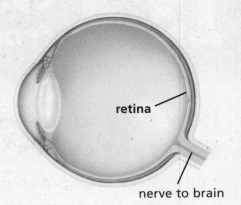

retina

nerve to brain

The retina is a layer of cells along the inside of the eye. Its cells detect light and send signals to the brain.

 **INSTANT REPLAY** What are two kinds of light-detecting cells in the retina?

_____

_____

What are all the different colors that you can see?

The rainbow of colors that humans can see are different frequencies between red and violet. Recall that humans see the lowest frequencies of light as red. The highest frequencies look violet.

Cone cells are the cells in your eyes that let you see color. Your eyes have three types of cone cells. Each type of cone cell absorbs a different range of light frequencies.

- "Red" cones absorb red light best, but also frequencies of yellow and green light.

- "Green" cones absorb green light best. They absorb a range from yellow through cyan. Cyan (SY-AN) is blue-green or green-blue.

- "Blue" cones absorb the blue end of the spectrum best.

Activity

Color Mixing
See student text, page 480.

The different combinations of red, green, and blue light allow your brain to see any color. These three colors are the primary colors of light. If you look closely at a television or computer screen, you will see tiny dots of red, green, and blue. Different combinations of these lights are used to make a color picture.

Visual Connection
See how the primary colors of light blend in the student text, page 478.

- When your RED and GREEN cones send signals, you see YELLOW.

- When your GREEN and BLUE cones send signals, you see CYAN.

- When your RED and BLUE cones send signals, you see MAGENTA—a dark pink or purple color.

- RED, GREEN, and BLUE signals together seem WHITE.

What are the three primary colors of light?

_____ _____ _____

Objects absorb some frequencies of light and reflect other frequencies. The frequencies that an object reflects make the color that you see. For example, a green leaf reflects mostly green light. The other frequencies of light are absorbed by the leaf.

Most light sources give off many different frequencies at once. Most objects reflect many different frequencies at once. Thus, most of the colors you see are combinations of frequencies.

The sky looks blue because blue waves of light are not absorbed by the atmosphere.

What color would an object be if it reflected mostly red light? _____

SECTION 13.4

SUMMARIZE	VOCABULARY
1. Describe the structures in your eye that allow you to see color. _____ _____ _____ _____	Circle the term that completes each sentence. 2. **Rod cells / cone cells** detect light, but not colors. 3. **Rod cells / cone cells** let you see colors. 4. The rod cells and cone cells are found in the **cornea / retina**.

Vocabulary

For each pair of terms, explain how they are related.

1 visible light and **electromagnetic spectrum**

_____

2 rod cells and **cone cells**

_____

Reviewing Key Concepts

3 What three things must happen before you can see an object?

a. _____

b. _____

c. _____

the **BIG** idea

4 List the four ways that matter can interact with light.

a. _____

b. _____

c. _____

d. _____

Test Practice

5 When light goes through two different mediums, it

   A changes direction
   B becomes visible
   C absorbs energy
   D goes away

6 Which structure allows you to see in dim light?

   A the retina
   B the rod cells
   C the cone cells
   D the electromagnetic spectrum

CHAPTER
14 Optics

Images are produced by light in many ways.

Getting Ready to Learn

Review Concepts

- You see an object when light emitted by or reflected from it enters your eye.
- The speed of light may change in different mediums.
- Reflection and refraction are two ways that light interacts with materials.

Activity

How Does a Spoon Reflect Your Face? See student text, page 493.

Review Vocabulary

Draw a line to connect each word to its definition.

reflect   a layer of tissue at the back of the eye

refract   to change direction

retina   to bounce off

Preview Key Vocabulary

Following are some key vocabulary terms you will see in this chapter. When you reach each one, write the term's definition and sketch a picture in the box to help you remember it.

Term	Definition	Sketch
angle of incidence		
angle of reflection		
lens		
cornea		

SECTION 14.1

Key Concept

Light tends to travel in straight lines.

Student text pages 495–499

What is optics?

Optics (AHP-tihks) is the science of light and vision. Optics is also the use of knowledge about visible light to develop optical tools. Eyeglasses, cameras, mirrors, magnifying lenses, binoculars, and telescopes are all optical tools.

Light travels in a straight line, unless the material, or medium, that it is traveling through changes. Light may change direction when there is a change in medium.

Activity

Reflection
See student text, page 495.

CLASSZONE.COM

Visualization See reflection in action.

How do mirrors reflect light?

Light reflects, or bounces off, a mirror in a predictable* way. The light bounces off the mirror at the same angle that the light hits the mirror. These two angles are called the angle of incidence and the angle of reflection.

The **angle of incidence** is the angle at which the light comes in. The **angle of reflection** is the angle at which the light bounces off. You can see these angles in the picture.

When light hits a mirror or a smooth surface, the angle of incidence is always equal to the angle of reflection. You can measure these angles by starting at an imaginary line called the normal. The normal is a line perpendicular to the surface and between the two angles.

Activity

The Law of Reflection
See student text, page 498.

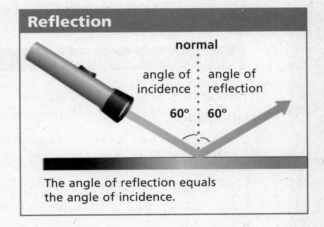

Reflection

normal

angle of incidence | angle of reflection

60° | 60°

The angle of reflection equals the angle of incidence.

INSTANT REPLAY

If light hits a mirror at an angle of incidence of 30 degrees, what would be the angle of reflection?

_____

*Academic Vocabulary: **Predictable** means that you expect something to happen in the same way each time. You might **predict** that you will sing the birthday song at every birthday party.

How do flat and curved mirrors form images?

Your reflection in a mirror is an image. In optics, an **image** is a picture of an object that is formed by light. The object is the actual thing itself. The image is the reflection of the object. Mirrors of different shapes make different kinds of images.

Flat Mirrors

An object's image is formed in a mirror when light bounces off the object and then off the mirror. The picture shows light being reflected off a bird and hitting a mirror.

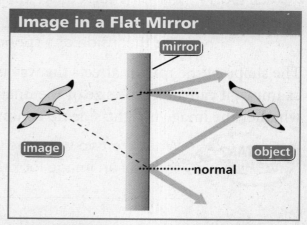

Image in a Flat Mirror

Light rays reflect off of an object and then off of the mirror. This forms the image.

Think about your image when you look into a flat mirror. Your image is right side up—your head is at the top. Your image looks as far from the mirror as you are standing. You look to your left to see the image of your left arm. However, you see the image as a person facing you, so your left arm looks like your image's right arm.

Curved Mirrors

If a mirror is flat, then the rays that hit the mirror will all reflect at the same angle. But if the mirror is curved, then the light rays will each hit the mirror at a different angle of incidence. Because the light rays have different angles of incidence, they will have different angles of reflection. As a result, your image in the mirror will look larger or smaller than you really are. A curved mirror may be convex or concave.

- A concave mirror is curved inward, like the inside of a spoon. Light rays get reflected in toward each other. Then they cross and move apart. The place where the rays cross is the mirror's **focal point.**

- A convex mirror is curved outward, like the outside of a spoon. Light rays are reflected out, so that they spread out.

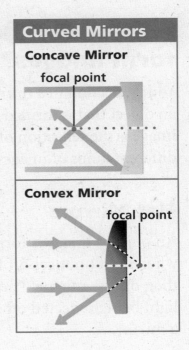

Curved Mirrors

Concave Mirror

focal point

Convex Mirror

focal point

Fill in the blanks: A _____ mirror is curved like the outside of a spoon, and a _____ mirror is curved like the inside of a spoon.

The shape of the mirror affects the way an image looks. For example, it can affect the size of the image. It can also affect whether the image is right-side up or upside down.

What are two ways the shape of a mirror can affect the way an image looks? _____

_____

SECTION 14.1	
SUMMARIZE	**VOCABULARY**
1. Draw a picture that explains the law of reflection. In your picture, label the angle of incidence, angle of reflection, and the normal.	Circle the correct phrase to answer each question. 2. What is the angle at which light bounces off a mirror—the **angle of incidence** or the **angle of reflection?** 3. What happens when light bounces off a mirror—is it **reflected** or **refracted?**

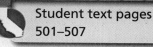
Student text pages
501–507

What causes light to refract?

When light refracts, it means the direction of light rays changes. Light changes direction when light rays change speed. The speed of light is different in different mediums. For example, light rays travel slower in glass and water than in air. So light can change speed and refract if it moves from one medium into another.

When light hits glass at any angle, it slows down and refracts. Scientists can predict how much light will refract. They can use this knowledge to make tools that control refraction.

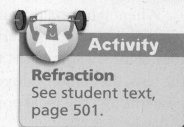

Activity

Refraction
See student text, page 501.

 What two things happen if light hits a glass at an angle?

_____   _____

What are lenses?

When you look into a flat mirror, your image looks normal. But curved mirrors can make your image look different. Curved glass can also change the way your eyes see objects. The glass does this by refracting light. Curved glass that refracts light is called a **lens.**

Like mirrors, lenses can be convex or concave. A convex lens is curved outward on both sides. A concave lens is curved inward on both sides. Different lenses refract light in different ways. Cameras, microscopes, telescopes, eyeglasses, magnifying glasses, and other tools all use lenses.

Visual Connection
See convex and concave images made by lenses in the student text, pages 506-507.

Mark It Up
Circle the lens that is convex. Draw a box around the lens that is concave.

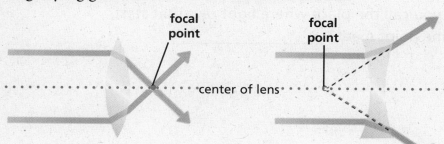

A convex lens causes these light rays to meet at a focal point.

A concave lens causes these light rays to spread out.

Convex Lenses

Cameras and magnifying glasses use convex lenses. Convex lenses can produce images that are smaller or larger than the object itself. The size of the image depends on the object's distance from the lens.

When light rays that are moving in the same direction refract through a convex lens, they come together. First the light rays enter the lens, they change direction. Then they pass through the focal point.

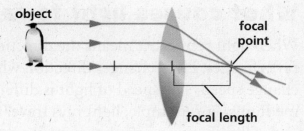

Light rays that came from the same direction cross at the focal point.

Look at the picture and find the focal point. It is the place behind the lens where light rays cross. The light that bounces straight off the penguin's feet can pass through the center of the lens without changing direction because it does not hit the lens at an angle. The distance from the center of the lens to the focal point is called the **focal length.** Focal lengths are marked on the drawing above.

 How many focal lengths are marked on the picture above? _____

Remember that there are many light rays bouncing off an object in different directions. These different light rays pass through the lens, and the lens refracts the light rays. The image forms where the light rays meet. The second drawing shows the path of two light rays that bounce off the penguin's head.

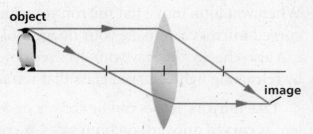

Light rays that bounce off the same object from different directions cross where the image is.

 What do you call the place where light rays that start at the same point meet? _____

The penguin in the picture is more than two focal lengths away from the center of the lens. When an object is this far from the lens, the image is smaller than the object. The lens also refracts the light rays so that the image is upside down. This is what happens when you use a camera. If you put a piece of film where the image is, the light will produce the image on the film. You will have a picture of a penquin.

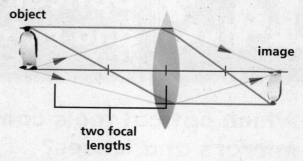

object

image

two focal lengths

The penguin's image is upside down and smaller than the actual penguin. This happens because the penguin is far away from the lens.

Remember that the way an image looks depends on how far away the object is from the lens. If an object is close to the lens—between one and two focal lengths—then the image will be larger than the object and right-side up. This is how a magnifying glass works. But if the object is more than two focal lengths away from the lens—such as the penguin in the drawing above—then the image is smaller and upside down.

🔵 **CLASSZONE.COM**

Simulation Work with convex and concave lenses to form images.

What are two tools that use convex lenses?

_____

SECTION 14.2

SUMMARIZE	VOCABULARY
1. An object is more than two focal lengths away from a convex lens. Describe how large or small the image will look. Will it be right-side up or upside down? _____ _____	Fill in each blank with the correct term from the list. **focal length** **lens** 2. Curved glass that refracts light is called a _____. 3. The distance from the center of a lens to the focal point is the _____.

Student text pages
510–516

Which optical tools combine mirrors and lenses?

Have you ever used two mirrors to see the back of your head? With two mirrors, you can have a different point of view than with one mirror. Two or more lenses can also be combined to make useful tools. Microscopes and telescopes, for example, are two optical tools that combine lenses.

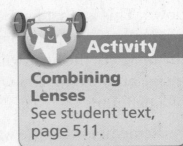

Activity

Combining Lenses
See student text, page 511.

Microscopes

A microscope is an optical tool that lets you see objects that are too small to see with your eyes alone. A regular light microscope combines convex lenses. One lens is close to the object. The image formed by this lens becomes the object for the second lens—the lens that you look through. Both lenses help make the image you see bigger.

Tiny objects do not reflect much light. Most microscopes use a lamp or mirror to shine more light onto or through the object.

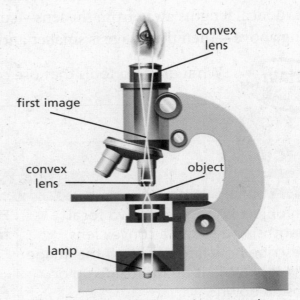

convex lens

first image

convex lens

object

lamp

These two convex lenses work together to enlarge the object.

INSTANT REPLAY

What kind of lenses do microscopes use?

_____

Mark It Up

Circle the two lenses in the drawing of the microscope.

Telescopes

A telescope is an optical tool that allows you to see objects that are too far away to see well with just your eyes. Some telescopes use a combination of lenses. Other telescopes use a combination of lenses and mirrors. The drawing below shows a telescope that uses two mirrors.

Visual Connection
See Microscopes and Telescopes in the student text, page 513.

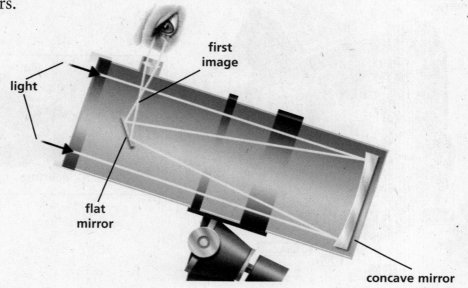

first
image

light

flat
mirror

concave mirror

What is a telescope? Underline the sentence that tells you.

How do cameras and other optical tools control light?

Optical tools control light in different ways. For example, optical tools may have parts that control the amount or direction of light.

Cameras

A camera records an image on film. A camera lets light in through a hole called an **aperture.** Most cameras have a part called an iris that forms the aperture. The iris can be changed so that the aperture is larger or smaller. The size of the aperture affects the way the image looks.

The iris of the camera works together with a lens. The lens is usually a convex lens. Light rays are refracted by the lens and pass through the aperture. This forms an image that is smaller than the object you are taking a picture of. The image is also upside down.

Look at the picture of how a traditional camera works. Light bounces off an object. The light passes into the lens, which refracts the light. The light rays cross in the aperture. The image is recorded at the back of the camera on film. The film absorbs the light. When the film is taken out and treated with chemicals, the image, or picture is revealed.

Film Camera

 Circle the word that completes the sentence: When light rays move through a camera lens, they are **reflected/refracted.**

SECTION 14.3

SUMMARIZE	VOCABULARY
1. What are two optical tools that use more than one lens? _____ _____ _____	camera aperture lens 2. Which tool makes an image by focusing light onto film? _____ 3. Which tool can refract light so that the light is focused into one spot? _____ 4. Which part of a camera is the opening that lets light through to the film? _____

The eye is a natural optical tool.

Student text pages 518–522

How does the eye focus light?

The human eye is similar to a camera in several ways. Both have lenses and irises. Both refract light to make a smaller, upside-down image. Look at the picture. It shows how light moves through the eye.

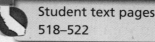

Activity

The Eye
See student text, page 520.

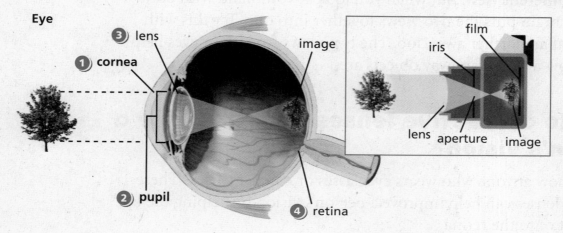

Eye

③ lens
① cornea
② pupil
④ retina
image

film
iris
lens   aperture   image

1. Light enters the eye through a clear membrane called the **cornea** (KAWR-nee-uh). Light is refracted by the cornea.

2. Light then passes through an opening called the **pupil.** The pupil and the iris control the amount of light that gets into the eye.

3. Light enters the lens. The lens refracts the light more.

4. Next, light passes through the center of the eye and forms an image on the retina. The retina sends signals to the brain.

INSTANT REPLAY

What are two structures in the eye refract light?

_____   _____

How do the eyes and brain work together?

The image on your retina is upside down. Your brain receives the signals from the retina and interprets them. This lets you see the world as right-side up. Together, your brain and eyes let you see bright and dark, color, shape, motion, and other patterns.

Your two eyes give you two slightly different views of the world. Hold your hand up close to your face. First, look at your hand with both eyes. Then look at your hand with one eye at a time. Each eye has a slightly different view. But when you look at your hand with both eyes, your brain puts the two views together into one. Try this with objects that are farther away, too. The two views from your eyes help you tell how near or far away objects are.

How do corrective lenses help improve a person's vision?

Do you know anyone who wears eyeglasses or contact lenses? These corrective lenses can help improve a person's vision by helping the eye focus light onto the retina.

The lenses in eyeglasses can refract light so that the light waves enter the eye differently. Corrective lenses may be convex or concave.

Look at the drawing. It shows how light moves into the eye of a person who is nearsighted. People who are nearsighted can best see objects that are nearby. When objects are far away, the image does not fall onto the retina. A concave lens can help focus the image onto the retina.

In nearsighted eyes, the image of a far-away object falls in front of the retina.

 **INSTANT REPLAY** Which type of lens can correct images for a nearsighted eye—a convex or concave lens?

_____

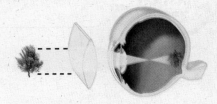

A concave lens causes light rays to move apart so that the image falls right on the retina.

Now look at the drawing here. It shows how light moves into the eye of a farsighted person. People who are farsighted can best see images that are farther away. However, images of objects that are near to them fall behind the retina. A convex lens can help focus the image onto the retina.

In farsighted eyes, the image of a close object falls behind the retina.

 **INSTANT REPLAY** Which type of lens can correct images for a nearsighted eye—a convex or concave lens?

_____

A convex lens bends light rays inward so that the image falls right on the retina.

SECTION 14.4	
SUMMARIZE	**VOCABULARY**
1. The human eye refracts light to form a smaller, upside-down image on the back of the eye. Where in the eye is light refracted? _____ _____ _____ _____	Draw a line to connect each word to its definition. **2.** pupil **a.** refracts light behind the pupil **3.** retina **b.** the front of the eye **4.** lens **c.** where an image falls **5.** cornea **d.** an opening formed by the iris

Vocabulary Fill in each blank with the correct words from the box.

1 A picture of an object that is formed by light is a(n)
   _____.

2 A clear tool that refracts light is a(n) _____.

3 The place behind a lens where rays of light cross is the
   _____.

4 The distance from the lens to the place behind the lens where
   light rays cross is the _____.

| focal point |
| focal length |
| lens |
| image |

Reviewing Key Concepts

5 Look at the picture. Label the *angle of incidence*,
   the *angle of reflection,* and the *normal.* How are
   the angle of incidence and the angle of reflection
   related? _____

6 When light passes through a lens, it refracts. What
   does this mean? _____

40° 40°

the **BIG** idea

7 Describe how light moves through the eye to form an image. In your
   answer, use the following terms: *cornea, pupil, lens,* and *retina.*

   _____

   _____

Test Practice

8 If the angle of incidence of a light
   ray is _____, the angle of
   reflection will be 70 degrees.

   A 50 degrees
   B 60 degrees
   C 70 degrees
   D 80 degrees

9 What happens to light waves
   when they pass through different
   mediums?

   A They stay the same.
   B They change direction and speed.
   C They change color.
   D They become straighter.

Glossary

A

absolute age
The actual age in years of an event or object. (p. 61)

> **edad absoluta** La edad real en años de un evento u objeto.

absorb
To take in. When a medium absorbs light, the light ceases to exist, and the medium gains the energy that was carried by the light. (p. 170)

> **absorber** Tomar, captar. Cuando un medio absorbe luz, la luz cesa de existir y el medio se beneficia de la energía que era llevada por la luz.

active transport
The process of using energy to move materials through a membrane. (p. 28)

> **transporte activo** El proceso de usar energía para mover sustancias a través de una membrana.

adaptation
An inherited trait that makes a species able to survive and reproduce in a particular environment. (p. 76)

> **adaptación** Cualquier rasgo heredado que permite a una especie sobrevivir o reproducirse en un medioambiente.

allele (uh-LEEL)
One form of a gene for a specific trait or gene product. (p. 46)

> **alelo** Una de las varias formas de un gen para un rasgo específico o un producto del gen.

ancestor
A distant or early form of an organism from which later forms descend. (p. 81)

> **ancestro** Una forma distante o temprana de un orga-nismo a partir de la cual descienden formas posteriores.

angle of incidence
The angle from the normal at which light comes in to a surface. (p. 182)

> **ángulo de incidencia** La forma del ángulo en el cual surge la luz a la superficie.

angle of reflection
The angle from the normal of light after bouncing. (p. 182)

> **ángulo de reflexión** El ángulo de donde rebota lo normal de la luz.

aperture
An opening, such as one that limits the amount of light from each part of an object. (p. 189)

> **apertura** Una apertura como una que limite la cantidad de luz de cada parte de un objeto.

appendicular skeleton (AP-uhn-DIHK-yuh-luhr)
The bones of the skeleton that function to allow movement, such as arm and leg bones. (p. 132)

> **esqueleto apendicular** Los huesos del esqueleto cuya función es permitir el movimiento, como los huesos del brazo y los huesos de la pierna.

artery
A blood vessel with strong walls that carries blood away from the heart. (p. 151)

> **arteria** Un vaso sanguíneo con paredes fuertes que lleva la sangre del corazón hacia otras partes del cuerpo.

asexual reproduction
The process by which a single organism produces offspring that have the same genetic material. (p. 39)

> **reproducción asexual** El proceso mediante el cual un solo organismo produce crías que tienen el mismo material genético.

atmosphere (AT-muh-SFEER)
The outer layer of gases of a large body in space, such as a planet or star; the mixture of gases that surrounds the solid Earth; one of the four parts of the Earth system.

> **atmósfera** La capa externa de gases de un gran cuerpo que se encuentra en el espacio, como un planeta o una estrella; la mezcla de gases que rodea la Tierra sólida; una de las cuatro partes del sistema terrestre.

atom
The smallest particle of an element that has the chemical properties of that element.

> **átomo** La partícula más pequeña de un elemento que tiene las propiedades químicas de ese elemento.

axial skeleton
The central part of the skeleton, which includes the skull, the spinal column, and the ribs. (p. 132)

> **esqueleto axial** La parte central del esqueleto que incluye el cráneo, la columna vertebral y las costillas.

B

bacteria (bak-TEER-ee-uh)
A large group of one-celled organisms that sometimes cause disease. Bacteria is a plural word; the singular is bacterium. (p. 5)

> **bacterias** Un grupo grande de organismos unicelulares que algunas veces causan enfermedades.

binary fission
A form of asexual reproduction by which some single-celled organisms reproduce. The genetic material is copied, and one cell divides into two independent cells that are each a copy of the original cell. Prokaryotes such as bacteria reproduce by binary fission. (p. 40)

> **fisión binaria** Una forma asexual de reproducción mediante la cual algunos organismos unicelulares se reproducen. El material genético se copia y una célula se divide en dos células independientes las cuales son copias de la célula original. Los organismos procariotas, tales como las bacterias, se reproducen mediante fisión binaria.

binomial nomenclature
(by-NOH-mee-uhl NOH-muhn-KLAY-chuhr)
The two-part naming system used to identify species. The first part of the name is the genus, and the second part of the name is the species. (p. 89)

> **nomenclatura biológica** El sistema de denominación de dos partes que se usa para identificar a las especies. La primera parte del nombre es el género y la segunda parte del nombre es la especie.

biodiversity
The number and variety of living things found on Earth or within an ecosystem.

> **biodiversidad** La cantidad y variedad de organismos vivos que se encuentran en la Tierra o dentro de un ecosistema.

biosphere (BY-uh-SFEER)
All living organisms on Earth in the air, on the land, and in the waters; one of the four parts of the Earth system.

> **biosfera** Todos los organismos vivos de la Tierra, en el aire, en la tierra y en las aguas; una de las cuatro partes del sistema de la Tierra.

C

capillary
A narrow blood vessel that connects arteries with veins. (p. 152)

> **capilar** Un vaso sanguíneo angosto que conecta a las arterias con las venas.

carbohydrate (KAHR-boh-HY-DRAYT)
A type of molecule made up of subunits of sugars and used for energy and structure. (p. 17)

> **carbohidrato** Un tipo de molécula compuesta de unidades de azúcares y usada como fuente de energía y como material estructural.

cardiac muscle
The involuntary muscle that makes up the heart. (p. 136)

> **músculo cardíaco** El músculo involuntario del que está hecho el corazón.

cartilage
A type of connective tissue that is tough but flexible. (p. 133)

> **cartílago** Un tipo de tejido conectivo que es fuerte y flexible.

cell
The smallest unit that is able to perform the basic functions of life.

> **célula** La unidad más pequeña capaz de realizar las funciones básicas de la vida.

cell cycle
The normal sequence of growth, maintenance, and division in a cell. (p. 35)

> **ciclo celular** La secuencia normal de crecimiento, mantenimiento y división en una célula.

cell membrane
The outer boundary of the cytoplasm, a layer that controls what enters or leaves the cell; a protective covering enclosing an entire cell. (p. 6)

> **membrana celular** El límite exterior del citoplasma, una capa que controla lo que entra y sale de la célula, una cubierta protectora que encierra una célula entera.

cell theory
Theory that every living thing is made of one or more cells; cells carry out the functions needed to support life; and cells come from other living cells. (p. 4)

> **teoría celular** La teoría de que todo ser viviente está hecho de una o más células; las células ejercen las funciones necesarias para sostener la vida; las células vienen de otras células vivas.

cell wall
A protective outer covering that lies just outside the cell membrane of plant cells. (p. 8)

pared celular Una cubierta exterior protectora que se encuentra justo fuera de la membrana celular de las células vegetales.

cellular respiration
A process in which cells use oxygen to release energy stored in sugars. (p. 24)

respiración celular Un proceso en el cual las células usan oxígeno para liberar energía almacenada en las azúcares.

chemical energy
Energy that is stored in the chemical composition of matter. The amount of chemical energy in a substance depends on the types and arrangement of its atoms. When wood or gasoline burns, chemical energy produces heat. The energy used by the cells in your body comes from chemical energy in the foods you eat. (p. 21)

energía química Energía almacenada en la composición química de la materia. La cantidad de energía química en una sustancia depende de los tipos y la disposición de sus átomos. Cuando se quema madera o gasolina, la energía química produce calor. La energía usada por las células en tu cuerpo proviene de la energía química en los alimentos que comes.

chemical reaction
The process by which chemical changes occur. In a chemical reaction, atoms are rearranged, and chemical bonds are broken and formed. (p. 17)

reacción química El proceso mediante el cual ocurren cambios químicos. En una reacción química, se reacomodan átomos y se rompen y se forman enlaces químicos.

chlorophyll (KLAWR-uh-fihl)
A light-absorbing chemical, a pigment, that traps the energy in sunlight and converts it to chemical energy. Found in chloroplasts of plant cells and the cells of other photosynthetic organisms. (p. 22)

clorofila Una sustancia química que absorbe luz, un pigmento, que atrapa la energía de la luz solar y la convierte a energía química. Se encuentra en los cloroplastos de células vegetales y en las células de otros orga-nismos fotosintéticos.

chloroplast (KLAWR-uh-PLAST)
An organelle in a plant cell that contains chlorophyll, a chemical that uses the energy from sunlight to make sugar. (p. 9)

cloroplasto Un organelo en una célula vegetal que contiene clorofila, una sustancia química que usa la energía de la luz solar para producir azúcar.

chromosome
The physical structure in a cell that contains the cell's genetic material. (p. 33)

cromosoma Una estructura corporal en la célula que contiene el material genético de la célula.

circulatory system
The group of organs, consisting of the heart and blood vessels, that circulates blood through the body.

sistema circulatorio El grupo de órganos, que consiste del corazón y los vasos sanguíneos, que hace circular la sangre por el cuerpo.

cladogram
A branching diagram of relationships among organisms; it is based on characteristics that are passed down from common ancestors. (p. 93)

cladograma Un diagrama de ramificación entre organismos; se basa en las características heredadas de antepasados comunes.

classification
The systematic grouping of different types of organisms by their shared characteristics. (p. 90)

clasificación La agrupación sistemática de diferentes tipos de organismos en base a las características que comparten.

compound
A substance made up of two or more different types of atoms bonded together.

compuesto Una sustancia formada por dos o más diferentes tipos de átomos enlazados.

cone cell
Cone-shaped cells in the retina that allow the eye to detect colors. (p. 178)

célula cónica Células en la retina en forma de cono que permiten al ojo detectar colores.

converge
To come together.

converger Reunirse

cornea (KAWR-nee-uh)
A transparent membrane that covers the front of the eye. (p. 191)

córnea Una membrana transparente que cubre el ojo.

cycle

n. A series of events or actions that repeat themselves regularly; a physical and/or chemical process in which one material continually changes locations and/or forms. Examples include the water cycle, the carbon cycle, and the rock cycle.

v. To move through a repeating series of events or actions.

ciclo Una serie de eventos o acciones que se repiten regularmente; un proceso físico y/o químico en el cual un material cambia continuamente de lugar y/o forma. Ejemplos: el ciclo del agua, el ciclo del carbono y el ciclo de las rocas.

cytokinesis (sy-toh-kuh-NEE-sihs)

The division of a parent cell's cytoplasm following mitosis. (p. 35)

citocinesis La división del citoplasma de la célula madre después de la mitosis.

cytoplasm (SY-tuh-PLAZ-uhm)

A thick, gelatin-like material contained within the cell membrane. Most of the work of the cell is carried out in the cytoplasm. (p. 6)

citoplasma Un material espeso, parecido a la gelatina, contenido dentro de la membrana celular. La mayor parte del trabajo de la célula se realiza en el citoplasma.

D

data

Information gathered by observation or experimentation that can be used in calculating or reasoning. *Data* is a plural word; the singular is *datum*.

datos Información reunida mediante observación o experimentación y que se puede usar para calcular o para razonar.

decibel dB

The unit used to measure the loudness of a sound wave. (p. 166)

decibel La unidad que se usa para medir el volumen de una onda sonora.

density

A property of matter representing the mass per unit volume.

densidad Una propiedad de la materia que representa la masa por unidad de volumen.

derived characteristic

A trait that has changed from its ancestral condition through evolution. (p. 93)

características derivadas Una característica que ha cambiado desde su condición ancestral a través de la evolución.

dichotomous key (dy-KAHT-uh-muhs)

An identification tool that gives a series of choices, each with only two possibilities.

clave dicótoma Una herramienta de identificación que ofrece una serie de opciones, cada una con sólo dos posibilidades.

diffuse

To cause to go in many different directions. (p. 175)

difuso Hacer que vaya en muchas direcciones diferentes.

diffusion (dih-FYOO-zhuhn)

The tendency of a substance to move from an area of higher concentration to an area of lower concentration. (p. 26)

difusión La tendencia de una sustancia a moverse de un área de mayor concentración a un área de menor concentración.

diverge

To move apart.

desviar Moverse por separado.

DNA

The genetic material found in all living cells that contains the information needed for an organism to grow, maintain itself, and reproduce. Deoxyribonucleic acid (dee-AHK-see-RY-boh-noo-KLEE-ihk). (p. 32)

ADN El material genético que se encuentra en todas las células vivas y que contiene la información necesaria para que un organismo crezca, se mantenga a sí mismo y se reproduzca. Ácido desoxiribunucleico.

domain

One of three divisions in a classification system based on different types of cells. The six kingdoms of living things are grouped into three domains: Archaea, Bacteria, and Eukarya.

dominio Una de las tres divisiones en un sistema de clasificación basado en los diferentes tipos de células. Los seis reinos de los organismos vivos esta agrupados en tres dominios: Archaea, Bacteria y Eukarya.

dominant

A term that describes the allele that determines the phenotype of an individual organism when two different copies are present in the genotype. (p. 47)

dominante Un término que describe al alelo que determina el fenotipo de un organismo cuando están presentes dos copias diferentes en el genotipo.

E

eardrum

A thin, tightly stretched membrane that separates the outer ear from the middle ear. (p. 164)

tambor del oído, tímpano Una delgada membrana, apretadamente estirada, que separa el oído exterior del oído medio.

egg

A female reproductive cell (gamete) that forms in the female reproductive organs and has just a single copy of the genetic material of the parent. (p. 51)

óvulo Una célula reproductiva femenina (gameto) que se forma en los órganos reproductivos de una hembra y tiene una sola copia del material genético de la madre.

electromagnetic spectrum EM spectrum

The range of all electromagnetic frequencies, including the following types (from lowest to highest frequency): radio waves, microwaves, infrared light, visible light, ultraviolet light, x-rays, and gamma rays. (p. 171)

espectro electromagnético La escala de todas las frecuencias electromagnéticas, incluyendo los siguientes tipos (de la frecuencia más baja a la más alta): ondas de radio, microondas, luz infrarroja, luz visible, luz ultravioleta, rayos X y rayos gamma.

electromagnetic wave EM wave

A type of wave, such as a light wave or radio wave, that does not require a material medium to travel; a disturbance that transfers energy through a field. (p. 170)

onda electromagnética Un tipo de onda, como una onda luminosa o de radio, que no requiere un medio material para propagarse; una perturbación que transfiere energía a través de un campo.

element

A substance that cannot be broken down into a simpler substance by ordinary chemical changes. An element consists of atoms of only one type.

elemento Una sustancia que no puede descomponerse en otra sustancia más simple por medio de cambios químicos normales. Un elemento consta de átomos de un solo tipo.

embryo (EHM-bree-OH)

A multicellular organism, plant or animal, in its earliest stages of development. (p. 122)

embrión Una planta o un animal en su estado mas temprano de desarrollo.

emigration

In population studies, the movement of individuals out of an ecosystem. (p. 79)

emigración En estudios poblacionales, el movimiento de individuos fuera de un ecosistema.

emit

To give off. (p. 173)

emitir Transmitir

endoskeleton

An internal support system typically made of bone, cartilage, ligament, and tendon tissues. It is a distinguishing characteristic of vertebrate animals. (p. 111)

endoesqueleto Un sistema de soporte interno, típicamente constituido de hueso, cartílago, ligamentos y tendones. Es una característica distintiva de los animales vertebrados.

energy

The ability to do work or to cause a change. For example, energy of a moving bowling ball knocks over pins; energy from food allows animals to move and to grow; and energy from the Sun heats Earth's surface and atmosphere, which causes air to move.

energía La capacidad para trabajar o causar un cambio. Por ejemplo, la energía de una bola de boliche en movimiento tumba los pinos; la energía proveniente de su alimento permite a los animales moverse y crecer; la energía del Sol calienta la superficie y la atmósfera de la Tierra, lo que ocasiona que el aire se mueva.

environment

Everything that surrounds a living thing. An environment is made up of both living and nonliving factors.

medio ambiente Todo lo que rodea a un organismo vivo. Un medio ambiente está compuesto de factores vivos y factores sin vida.

environmental factors

Conditions that affect survival, such as the food supply, predators, and disease.

factores medioambientales Condiciones que afectan la supervivencia, tales como el suministro de comida, predatores y enfermedades.

eukaryotic cell (yoo-KAR-ee-AHT-ihk)
A cell in which the genetic material is enclosed within a nucleus, surrounded by its own membrane. (p. 7)

célula eucariota Una célula en la cual el material genético esta dentro de un núcleo, rodeado por su propia membrana.

evolution
The process through which species change over time; can refer to the changes in a particular population or to the formation and extinction of species over the course of Earth's history. (p. 74)

evolución El proceso mediante el cual las especies cambian con el tiempo; puede referirse a cambios en una población en particular o a la formación y extinción de especies en el curso de la historia de la Tierra.

exoskeleton
The strong, flexible outer covering of some invertebrate animals, such as arthropods. (p. 111)

exoesqueleto La cubierta exterior fuerte y flexible de algunos animales invertebrados, como los artrópodos.

experiment
An organized procedure to study something under controlled conditions.

experimento Un procedimiento organizado para estudiar algo bajo condiciones controladas.

extinction
The permanent disappearance of a species. (p. 72)

extinción La desaparición permanente de una especie.

F

fermentation
A chemical process by which cells release energy from sugar when no oxygen is present. (p. 24)

fermentación Un proceso químico mediante el cual las células liberan energía del azúcar cuando no hay oxígeno presente.

fertilization
Part of the process of sexual reproduction in which a male reproductive cell and a female reproductive cell combine to make a new cell that can develop into a new organism. (pp. 52, 119)

fertilización El proceso mediante el cual una célula reproductiva masculina y una célula reproductiva femenina se combinan para formar una nueva célula que puede convertirse en un organismo nuevo.

fetus
The developing human embryo from eight weeks to birth. (p. 128)

feto El embrión humano en desarrollo de las ocho semanas al nacimiento.

fiber optics
Technology that uses transparent fibers to transmit light. This technology is often used in communications.

fibra óptica Tecnología que utiliza fibras transparentes para transmitir luz. Esta tecnología es utilizada frecuentemente en las comunicaciones.

field
An area around an object where the object can apply a force—such as gravitational force, magnetic force, or electrical force—on another object without touching it.

campo Un área alrededor de un objeto donde el objeto puede aplicar una fuerza, como fuerza gravitacional, fuerza magnética o fuerza eléctrica, sobre otro objeto sin tocarlo.

fluid
A substance that can flow easily, such as a gas or a liquid. (p. 148)

fluido Una sustancia que fluye fácilmente, como por ejemplo un gas o un líquido.

focal length
The distance from the center of a lens to its focal point. (p. 186)

distancia focal La distancia desde el centro de un lente hasta su punto focal.

focal point
The point at which parallel light rays come together after reflection from a mirror or refraction by a lens; the point at which parallel light rays appear to diverge from after reflection by a mirror or refraction by a lens. (p. 184)

punto focal El punto en el cual se unen los rayos paralelos de luz después de ser reflejados por un espejo o refractados por un lente; el punto en el cual los rayos paralelos de luz parecen desviarse después de ser reflejados por un espejo o refractados por un lente.

force
A push or a pull; something that changes the motion of an object. (p. 138)

fuerza Un empuje o un jalón; algo que cambia el movimiento de un objeto.

fossil
A trace or the remains of a once-living thing from long ago.

fósil Rastro o los restos de un ser viviente que vivió hace mucho años.

frequency

The number of cycles per unit time; can be measured by the number of waves that pass a fixed point in a given amount of time, usually one second. (p. 161)

> **frecuencia** El número de ciclos por unidad de tiempo; puede ser medido por el número de ondas que pasan por un punto fijo en un determinado tiempo, usualmente un segundo.

friction

A force that resists the motion between two surfaces in contact.

> **fricción** Una fuerza que resiste el movimiento entre dos superficies en contacto.

fruit

The ripened ovary of a flowering plant that contains the seeds. (p. 123)

> **fruta** El ovario maduro de una planta floreciente que contiene las semillas.

fulcrum

A fixed point around which a lever rotates. (p. 141)

> **fulcro** Un punto fijo alrededor del cual gira una palanca.

G

gamete

A sperm or egg cell, containing half the usual number of chromosomes of an organism (one chromosome from each pair), which is found only in the reproductive organs of an organism. (pp. 51, 119)

> **gameto** Un óvulo o un espermatozoide, que contiene la mitad del número usual de cromosomas de un organismo (un cromosoma de cada par), que se encuentra sólo en los órganos reproductivos de un organismo.

gene

The basic unit of heredity that consists of a segment of DNA on a chromosome. (p. 45)

> **gen** La unidad básica de herencia que consiste en un segmento de ADN en un cromosoma.

genetic material

The nucleic acid DNA that is present in all living cells and contains the information needed for a cell's growth, maintenance, and reproduction.

material genético El ácido nucleico ADN, que esta presente en todas las células vivas y que contiene la información necesaria para el crecimiento, el mantenimiento y la reproducción celular.

genetic variation

Differences in DNA in a population. (p. 76)

> **variación genética** Diferencias de ADN en la población.

genotype (JEHN-uh-TYP)

The genetic makeup of an organism; all the alleles that an organism has. (p. 47)

> **genotipo** La estructura genética de un organismo; todos los alelos que tiene un organismo.

genus

The first part of a binomial name that groups together closely related species. The genus Felis includes all species of small cats. (p. 89)

> **género** La primera parte de un nombre biológico que agrupa a especies muy relacionadas entre sí. El género Felis incluye a todas las especies de gatos pequeños.

geologic time scale

The summary of Earth's history, divided into intervals of time defined by major events or changes on Earth. (p. 64)

> **escala de tiempo geológico** El resumen de la historia de la Tierra, dividido en intervalos de tiempo definidos por los principales eventos o cambios en la Tierra.

geosphere (JEE-uh-SFEER)

All the features on Earth's surface—continents, islands, and seafloor—and everything below the surface—the inner and outer core and the mantle; one of the four parts of the Earth system.

> **geosfera** Todas las características de la superficie de la Tierra, es decir, continentes, islas y el fondo marino, y de todo bajo la superficie, es decir, el núcleo externo e interno y el manto; una de las cuatro partes del sistema de la Tierra.

gland

A group of specialized cells that produces a specific substance, such as a hormone. (p. 115)

> **glándula** Un grupo de células especializadas que produce una sustancia específica, como una hormona.

glucose

A sugar molecule that is a major energy source for most cells, produced by the process of photosynthesis. (p. 21)

> **glucosa** Una molécula de azúcar que es la principal fuente de energía para la mayoría de las células, producida mediante el proceso de fotosíntesis.

gravity

The force that objects exert on each other because of their mass.

> **gravedad** La fuerza que los objetos ejercen entre sí debido a su masa.

H

half-life
The length of time it takes for half of the nuclei in a sample of a radioactive element to change from an unstable form into another form. (p. 62)

> **vida media** El tiempo que tarda en cambiar la mitad de los núcleos de una muestra de un elemento radioactivo, de una forma inestable a otra.

heredity
The passing of genes from parents to offspring; the genes are expressed in the traits of the offspring. (p. 46)

> **herencia** La transferencia de genes de los progenitores a las crías; los genes se expresan en los rasgos de las crías.

hertz Hz
The unit used to measure frequency. One hertz is equal to one complete cycle per second. (p. 161)

> **hercio** La unidad usada para medir frecuencia. Un hercio es igual a un ciclo completo por segundo.

hibernation
A sleeplike state in which certain animals spend the winter. Hibernation reduces an animal's need for food and helps protect it from cold. (p. 104)

> **hibernación** Un estado parecido al de sueño en el cual ciertos animales pasan el invierno. La hibernación reduce la necesidad de alimento de un animal y le ayuda a protegerse del frío.

homeostasis (HOH-mee-oh-STAY-sihs)
A condition needed for health and functioning in which an organism or cell maintains a relatively stable internal environment. (p. 114)

> **homeostasis** Una condición necesaria para la salud y el funcionamiento en la cual un organismo o una cé-lula mantiene un medio ambiente estable e interna.

hormone
A chemical that is made in one organ, travels through the blood, and affects target cells. (p. 115)

> **hormona** Una sustancia química que se produce en un órgano y viaja por la sangre, afectando a las células en blanco de tiro.

hydrosphere (HY-druh-sfeer)
All water on Earth—in the atmosphere and in the oceans, lakes, glaciers, rivers, streams, and underground reservoirs; one of the four parts of the Earth system.

> **hidrosfera** Toda el agua de la Tierra: en la atmósfera y en los océanos, lagos, glaciares, ríos, arroyos y depósitos subterráneos; una de las cuatro partes del sistema de la Tierra.

hypothesis
A tentative explanation for an observation or phenomenon. A hypothesis is used to make testable predictions. (p. 94)

> **hipótesis** Una explicación provisional de una observación o de un fenómeno. Una hipótesis se usa para hacer predicciones que se pueden probar.

I

ice core
A cylindrical sample that shows the layers of snow and ice that have built up over the years. (p. 67)

> **núcleo de hielo** Una muestra cilíndrica que presenta las capas de nieve y hielo que se han acumulado con los años.

igneous rock (IHG-nee-uhs)
Rock that forms as molten rock cools and becomes solid.

> **roca ígnea** Roca que se forma al enfriarse la roca fundida y hacerse sólida.

image
A picture of an object formed by light. (p. 183)

> **imagen** Retrato de un objeto formado por rayos de luz.

immigration
In population studies, the movement of an organism into a range inhabited by individuals of the same species. (p. 78)

> **inmigración** En estudios poblacionales, el movimiento de un organismo hacia un territorio habitado por individuos de la misma especie.

index fossil
A fossil of an organism that was common, lived in many areas, and existed only during a certain span of time. Index fossils are used to help determine the age of rock layers. (p. 61)

> **fósil indicador** Un fósil de un organismo que era común, vivió en muchas áreas y existió sólo durante cierto período de tiempo. Los fósiles indicadores se usan para ayudar a determinar la edad de las capas de roca.

inner ear
The innermost part of the ear; it includes the semicircular canals and the cochlea. (p. 164)

> **oído interno** La parte interior del oído. Incluye canales semicirculares y la cóclea.

input force

The force exerted on a machine; it enables the machine to do work. (p. 142)

fuerza de la entrada La presión aplicada a una máquina; ayuda la máquina a funcionar para hacer el trabajo.

interaction

The condition of acting or having an influence upon something. Living things in an ecosystem interact with both the living and nonliving parts of their environment.

interacción La condición de actuar o influir sobre algo. Los organismos vivos en un ecosistema interactúan con las partes vivas y las partes sin vida de su medio ambiente.

interphase

The period in the cell cycle in which a cell grows, maintains itself, and prepares for division. (p. 35)

interfase El período en el ciclo celular en el cual una célula crece, se mantiene y se prepara para la división.

invertebrate

An animal that has no backbone. (p. 97)

invertebrado Un animal que no tiene columna vertebral.

J,K

joint

A place where two bones in the skeletal system meet. (p. 133)

coyuntura Un lugar donde se encuentran dos huesos en el sistema esquelético.

L

law

In science, a rule or principle describing a physical relationship that always works in the same way under the same conditions. The law of conservation of energy is an example.

ley En las ciencias, una regla o un principio que describe una relación física que siempre funciona de la misma manera bajo las mismas condiciones. La ley de la conservación de la energía es un ejemplo.

law of conservation of energy

A law stating that no matter how energy is transferred or transformed, it continues to exist in one form or another.

ley de la conservación de la energía Una ley que establece que no importa cómo se transfiere o transforma la energía, toda la energía sigue presente en alguna forma u otra.

lens

A transparent optical tool that refracts light. (p. 185)

lente Una herramienta óptica transparente que refracta la luz.

lever

A solid bar that rotates, or turns, around a fixed point (fulcrum); one of the six simple machines. (p. 141)

palanca Una barra sólida que da vueltas o gira alre-dedor de un punto fijo (el fulcro); una de las seis máquinas simples.

limiting factor

A factor or condition that prevents the continuing growth of a population in an ecosystem. (p. 78)

factor limitante Un factor o una condición que impide el crecimiento continuo de una población en un ecosistema.

lipid

A type of molecule made up of subunits of fatty acids. Lipids are found in the fats, oils, and waxes used for structure and to store energy. (p. 18)

lípido Un tipo de molécula compuesta de unidades de ácidos grasos. Los lípidos se encuentran en las grasas, los aceites y las ceras usadas como materiales estructurales y para almacenar energía.

M

mass

A measure of how much matter an object is made of.

masa Una medida de la cantidad de materia de la que está compuesto un objeto.

mass extinction

One of several periods in Earth's history when large numbers of species became extinct at nearly the same time. (p. 72)

extinción masiva Uno de varios períodos en la historia de la Tierra cuando grandes números de especies se extinguieron casi al mismo tiempo.

matter
Anything that has mass and volume. Matter exists ordinarily as a solid, a liquid, or a gas.

> **materia** Todo lo que tiene masa y volumen. Generalmente la materia existe como sólido, líquido o gas.

mechanical advantage
The number of times a machine multiplies the input force; output force divided by input force. (p. 142)

> **ventaja mecánica** El número de veces que una máquina multiplica la fuerza de entrada; la fuerza de salida dividida por la fuerza de entrada.

medium
A substance through which a wave moves. (p. 160)

> **medio** Una sustancia a través de la cual se mueve una onda.

meiosis (my-OH-sihs)
Process in which the nucleus of a cell divides in the production of haploid (n) cells, such as egg cells and sperm cells. Meiosis is a part of sexual reproduction and occurs only in reproductive cells. (p. 51)

> **meiosis** El proceso en el cual el núcleo de una célula se divide en la producción de células haploides, tales como óvulos y espermatozoides. La meiosis es una parte de la reproducción sexual y ocurre sólo en células reproductivas.

menstruation
A period of about five days during which blood and tissue exit the body through the vagina. (p. 126)

> **menstruación** Un período de aproximadamente cinco días durante el cual salen del cuerpo sangre y tejido por la vagina.

metamorphic rock (MEHT-uh-MAWR-fihk)
Rock formed as heat or pressure causes existing rock to change in structure, texture, or mineral composition.

> **roca metamórfica** Roca formada cuando el calor o la presión ocasionan que la roca existente cambie de estructura, textura o composición mineral.

microscope
An instrument that uses glass lenses to magnify an object. (p. 3)

> **microscopio** Un instrumento que usa lentes de vidrio para magnificar un objeto.

middle ear
The middle part of the ear; it includes three bones in an air-filled chamber and is connected to the throat by the eustachian tube. (p. 164)

> **oído medio** La parte media de oído; incluye tres huesos en una cavidad llena de aire y está conectada a la garganta por medio de la trompa de Eustaquio.

mitochondria (MY-tuh-KAWN-dree-uh)
Organelles that release energy by using oxygen to break down sugars. (p. 9)

> **mitocondrias** Organelos que liberan energía usando oxígeno para romper los azúcares.

mitosis
The phase in the cell cycle during which the nucleus divides. (p. 35)

> **mitosis** La fase en el ciclo celular durante la cual se divide el núcleo.

molecule
A group of atoms that are held together by covalent bonds so that they move as a single unit.

> **molécula** Un grupo de átomos que están unidos me-diante enlaces covalentes de tal manera que se mue-ven como una sola unidad.

mucus
A fluid produced by epithelial tissues in several parts of the body; it forms a protective coating. (p. 155)

> **mucosidad** Un fluido producido por los tejidos epiteliales en varias partes del cuerpo; forma una capa protectora.

multicellular organism
A term used to describe an organism that is made up of many cells. (pp. 3, 32)

> **multicelular** Un término usado para describir a un organismo que esta formado por muchas células.

muscular system
The muscles of the body that, together with the skeletal system, function to produce movement. (p. 135)

> **sistema muscular** Los músculos del cuerpo que, junto con el sistema óseo, sirven para producir movimiento.

N

natural selection
The process through which members of a species that are best suited to their environment survive and reproduce at a higher rate than other members of the species. (p. 75)

selección natural El proceso mediante el cual los miembros de una especie que están mejor adecuados a su medio ambiente sobreviven y se reproducen a una tasa más alta que otros miembros de la especie.

niche (nihch)
The role a living thing plays in its habitat. A plant is a food producer, whereas an insect both consumes food as well as provides food for other consumers.

nicho El papel que juega un organismo vivo en su hábitat. Una planta es un productor de alimento mientras que un insecto consume alimento y a la vez sirve de alimento a otros consumidores.

nucleic acid (noo-KLEE-ihk)
A type of molecule, made up of subunits of nucleotides, that is part of the genetic material of a cell and is needed to make proteins. DNA and RNA are nucleic acids. (p. 18)

ácido nucleico Un tipo de molécula, compuesto de unidades de nucleótidos, que es parte del material genético de una célula y se necesita para producir proteínas. El ADN y el ARN son ácidos nucleicos.

nucleus (NOO-klee-uhs)
The structure in a eukaryotic cell that contains the genetic material a cell needs to reproduce and function. (p. 7)

núcleo La estructura en una célula eucariota que contiene el material genético que la célula necesita para reproducirse y funcionar.

O

optics (AHP-tihks)
The study of light, vision, and related technology. (p. 182)

óptica El estudio de la luz, la visión y la tecnología relacionada a ellas.

organ
A structure that is made up of different tissues working together to perform a particular function. (pp. 12, 103)

órgano Una estructura compuesta de diferentes tejidos que trabajan juntos para realizar una función determinada.

organelle (AWR-guh-NEHL)
A structure in a cell that is enclosed by a membrane and that performs a particular function. (p. 7)

organelo Una estructura en una célula, envuelta en una membrana, que realiza una función determinada.

organism
An individual living thing, made up of one or many cells. (p. 103)

organismo Un ser, compuesto de una o muchas células.

organ system
A group of organs that together perform a function. (p. 103)

sistema de órganos Un grupo de órganos que juntos realizan una función.

original remains
A fossil that is the actual body or body parts of an organism. (p. 66)

restos originales Un fósil que es en realidad el cuerpo o partes del cuerpo de un organismo.

osmosis (ahz-MOH-sihs)
The diffusion of water through a membrane. (p. 27)

osmosis La difusión de agua a través de una membrana.

outer ear
The outermost part of the ear; it includes the part of the ear on the outside of the skull, the ear canal, and the eardrum. (p. 164)

oído externo La parte exterior del oído; incluye la parte que está fuera del cráneo, el canal del oído y el tímpano.

output force
The force that a machine exerts on an object. (p. 142)

fuerza de salida La fuerza que emplea la máquina en un objeto.

ovule
A structure in a female reproductive system that holds an immature egg cell. (p. 123)

óvulo Una estructura en el sistema reproductivo femenino que lleva la célula inmadura del huevo.

P, Q

passive transport
The movement of materials through a membrane without any input of energy. (p. 27)

transporte pasivo El movimiento de sustancias a través de una membrana sin aporte de energía.

phenotype
The observable characteristics or traits of an organism. (p. 47)

> **fenotipo** Las características o rasgos visibles de un organismo.

photosynthesis (FOH-toh-SIHN-thih-sihs)
The process by which green plants and other producers use simple compounds and energy from light to make sugar, an energy-rich compound. (p. 22)

> **fotosíntesis** El proceso mediante el cual las plantas verdes y otros productores usan compuestos simples y energía de la luz para producir azúcares, compuestos ricos en energía.

pitch
The quality of highness or lowness of a sound. Pitch is associated with the frequency of a sound wave—the higher the frequency, the higher the pitch. (p. 163)

> **tono** La cualidad de un sonido de ser alto o bajo. El tono está asociado con la frecuencia de una onda sonora: entre más alta sea la frecuencia, más alto es el tono.

placenta
An organ that transports materials between a pregnant female mammal and the offspring developing inside her body. (p. 128)

> **placenta** Un órgano que transporta sustancias entre un mamífero hembra preñado y la cría que se está desarrollando dentro de su cuerpo.

pollen
Tiny multicellular grains that contain the undeveloped sperm cells of a plant. (p. 122)

> **polen** Los diminutos granos multicelulares que contienen las células espermáticas sin desarrollar de una planta.

population
A group of organisms of the same species that live in the same area. For example, a desert will have populations of different species of lizards and cactus plants. (p. 75)

> **población** Un grupo de organismos de la misma especie que viven en la misma área. Por ejemplo, un desierto tendrá poblaciones de distintas especies de lagartijas y de cactus.

pressure
A measure of how much force is acting on a certain area; how concentrated a force is. Pressure is equal to the force divided by area. (p. 148)

> **presión** Una medida de cuánta fuerza actúa sobre cierta área; el nivel de concentración de la fuerza. La presión es igual a la fuerza dividida entre el área.

probability
The likelihood or chance that a specific outcome will occur out of a total number of outcomes. (p. 50)

> **probabilidad** La posibilidad de que ocurra un resultado específico en un número total de resultados.

prokaryotic cell (proh-KAR-ee-AWT-ihk)
A type of cell that lacks a nucleus and other organelles. Its DNA is in a single chromosome. (p. 7)

> **célula procariota** Una célula que carece de núcleo y otros organelos. Su ADN se encuentra en una sola cromosoma.

protein
One of many types of molecules made up of chains of amino acid subunits. Proteins control the chemical activity of a cell and support growth and repair. (p. 18)

> **proteína** Uno de muchos tipos de moléculas formadas por cadenas de aminoácidos. Las proteínas controlan la actividad química de una célula y sustentan el crecimiento y la reparación.

Punnett square
A chart used to show all the ways alleles from two parents can combine and be passed to offspring; used to predict all genotypes that are possible. (p. 49)

> **cuadro de Punnet** Una tabla que se usa para mostrar todas las formas en que los alelos de los progenitores pueden combinarse y pasarse a las crías; se usa para predecir todos los genotipos que son posibles.

pupil
The circular opening in the iris of the eye that controls how much light enters the eye. (p. 191)

> **pupila** La apertura circular en el iris del ojo que controla cuánta luz entra al ojo.

R

radiation (RAY-dee-AY-shuhn)
Energy that travels across distances in the form of electromagnetic waves.

> **radiación** Energía que viaja a través de la distancia en forma de ondas electromagnéticas.

recessive
A term that describes an allele that is not expressed when combined with a dominant form of the gene. (p. 47)

> **recesivo** Un término que describe un alelo que no se expresa cuando se combina con una forma dominante del gen.

reflect

To bounce or bounce off; a surface may reflect light; light may reflect after it strikes a surface. (p. 175)

reflejar Rebotar o rebotar de; una superficie puede rebotar la luz; la luz puede rebotar después de golpear una superficie.

refract

To change direction (of light) due to a change in speed; the surface between two mediums refracts light; light refracts as it encounters a change in medium. (p. 176)

refractar Cambio de dirección (de la luz) debido a cambio de velocidad; la superficie entre dos medios refracta la luz; la luz se refracta al encontrar cambios en el medio.

regeneration

In some organisms, the process by which certain cells produce new tissue growth at the site of a wound or lost limb; also a form of asexual reproduction. (p. 40)

regeneración En algunos organismos, el proceso mediante el cual ciertas células producen crecimiento de tejido nuevo en el sitio de una herida o de una extremidad perdida; también un tipo de reproducción asexual.

relative age

The age of an event or object in relation to other events or objects. (p. 58)

edad relativa La edad de un evento u objeto en relación a otros eventos u objetos.

replication

The process by which DNA is copied before it condenses into chromosomes. Replication takes place before a cell divides.

replicación El proceso mediante el cual el ADN se copia antes de condensarse en los cromosomas. La replicación se realiza antes de que una célula se divida.

retina (REHT-uhn-uh)

A light-sensitive tissue that lines the inside of the eye. (p. 178)

retina Un tejido, sensible a la luz, que forra la parte interna del ojo.

RNA

A molecule that carries genetic information from DNA to a ribosome, where the genetic information is used to bring together amino acids to form a protein. Ribonucleic acid (RY-boh-noo-KLEE-ihk).

ARN Una molécula que lleva información genética del ADN al ribosoma, donde la información genética se usa para unir aminoácidos para formar una proteína. Ácido ribonucleico.

rock cycle

The set of natural, repeating processes that form, change, break down, and re-form rocks. (p. 59)

ciclo de las rocas La serie de procesos naturales y repetitivos que forman, cambian, descomponen y vuelven a formar rocas.

rod cell

Long, thin cells located in the retina that let the eye detect dim light; also called rods. (p. 178)

células de Barra Células largas localizadas en la retina que permiten que el ojo detecte luz baja; también llamadas barras.

root system

The system in a plant that anchors the plant and generally provides for the exchange of materials with soil. (p. 107)

sistema de raíz El sistema en una planta que la ancla y generalmente suple el intercambio de materiales con terreno.

S

sedimentary rock (sehd-uh-MEHN-tuh-ree)

Rock formed as pieces of older rocks and other loose materials get pressed or cemented together or as dissolved minerals re-form and build up in layers.

roca sedimentaria Roca que se forma cuando los pedazos de rocas más viejas y otros materiales sueltos son presionados o cementados o cuando los minerales disueltos vuelven a formarse y se acumulan en capas.

seed

A plant embryo that is enclosed in a protective coating and has its own source of nutrients. (p. 122)

semilla El embrión de una planta que esta dentro de una cubierta protectora y que tiene su propia fuente de nutrientes.

semicircular canals

Fluid-filled chambers in the inner ear that help sense position and motion. (p. 155)

canales semicirculares Compartimientos de fluido en el oído interno que ayuda en la sensación de posición y movimiento.

sexual reproduction

A type of reproduction in which male and female reproductive cells combine to form offspring with genetic material from both cells. (p. 44)

reproducción sexual Un tipo de reproducción en el cual se combinan las células reproductivas femeninas y masculinas para formar una cría con material genético de ambas células.

shoot system

The system in a plant that includes structures for photosynthesis, support, storage, and the exchange of materials with the atmosphere; includes stems and leaves. (p. 107)

sistema de lanzamiento El sistema en una planta que incluye estructuras para fotosíntesis, apoyo, almacenaje y el intercambio de materias con la atmósfera; incluye pedúnculos y hojas.

simple machine

One of the basic machines on which all other mechanical machines are based. The six simple machines are the lever, inclined plane, wheel and axle, pulley, wedge, and screw. (p. 139)

máquina simple Una de las máquinas básicas sobre las cuales están basadas todas las demás máquinas mecánicas. Las seis máquinas simples son la palanca, el plano inclinado, la rueda y eje, la polea, la cuña y el tornillo.

skeletal muscle

A voluntary muscle that attaches to the skeleton. (p. 136)

músculo esquelético Un músculo voluntario que está sujeto al esqueleto.

skeletal system

The framework of bones that supports the body, protects internal organs, and anchors all the body's movement. (p. 132)

sistema óseo El armazón de huesos que sostiene al cuerpo, protege a los órganos internos y sirve de ancla para todo el movimiento del cuerpo.

smooth muscle

Muscle that performs involuntary movement and is found inside certain organs, such as the stomach. (p. 136)

músculo liso Músculos que realizan movimiento involuntario y se encuentran dentro de ciertos órganos, como el estómago.

sound

A pressure wave that is produced by a vibrating object and travels through matter. (p. 160)

sonido Un tipo de onda que es producida por un objeto que vibra y que viaja a través de la materia.

specialization

The specific organization of a cell and its structure that allows it to perform a specific function. (p. 11)

especialización La organización específica de una célula y de su estructura que le permite realizar una función específica.

speciation

The evolution of a new species from an existing species. (p. 77)

especiación La evolución de una nueva especie a partir de una especie existente.

species

A group of living things that are so closely related that they can breed with one another and produce offspring that can breed as well.

especie Un grupo de organismos que están tan estrechamente relacionados que pueden aparearse entre sí y producir crías que también pueden aparearse.

sperm

A male reproductive cell (gamete) that forms in the male reproductive organs and has just a single copy of the genetic material of the parent. (p. 52)

esperma Una célula reproductiva masculina (gameto) que se forma en los órganos reproductivos de un macho y tiene una sola copia del material genético del progenitor.

stomata

Openings in a plant's dermal tissue that control the exchange of water vapor, oxygen, and carbon dioxide with the atmosphere. (p. 105)

stomate Aperturas en los tejidos dermales de una planta, que controlan el intercambio de vapor de aguaoxígeno y dióxido de carbono con la atmósfera.

system

A group of objects or phenomena that interact. A system can be as simple as a rope, a pulley, and a mass. It also can be as complex as the interaction of energy and matter in the four parts of the Earth system.

sistema Un grupo de objetos o fenómenos que interactúan. Un sistema puede ser algo tan sencillo como una cuerda, una polea y una masa. También puede ser algo tan complejo como la interacción de la energía y la materia en las cuatro partes del sistema de la Tierra.

T

taxonomy
The science of classifying and naming organisms.

taxonomía La ciencia de clasificar y ponerle nombre a los organismos.

technology
The use of scientific knowledge to solve problems or engineer new products, tools, or processes.

tecnología El uso de conocimientos científicos para resolver problemas o para diseñar nuevos productos, herramientas o procesos.

theory
In science, a set of widely accepted explanations of observations and phenomena. A theory is a well-tested explanation that is consistent with all available evidence. (p. 81)

teoría En las ciencias, un conjunto de explicaciones de observaciones y fenómenos que es ampliamente aceptado. Una teoría es una explicación bien probada que es consecuente con la evidencia disponible.

tissue
A group of similar cells that are organized to do a specific job. (pp. 12, 103)

tejido Un grupo de células parecidas que juntas realizan una función específica en un organismo.

trait
1. A characteristic of an individual, such as a particular eye color; traits can be inherited or acquired.
2. Any type of feature that can be used to tell two species apart, such as size or bone structure.

rasgo 1. Característica de un individuo, tal como el color de los ojos; rasgos pueden ser heredados o adquiridos.
2. Cualquier característica que puede usarse para dife-renciar a dos especies, como el tamaño o la estructura ósea.

transmit
To let pass through. (p. 175)

transmitir Dejar pasar a través.

U

umbilical cord
A long tube in a pregnant female mammal that connects the developing offspring to the placenta. (p. 128)

cordón umbilical Un largo tubo en un mamífero femenino que conecta a la cría en desarrollo a la placenta.

unicellular organism
A term used to describe an organism that is made up of a single cell. (pp. 3, 32)

unicelular Un término usado para describir a un organismo que está compuesto de una sola célula.

uniformitarianism (YOO-nuh-FAWR-mih-TAIR-ee-uh-nihz-uhm)
A theory that processes shaping Earth today, such as erosion and deposition, also shaped Earth in the past, and that these processes cause large changes over geologic time. (p. 63)

uniformismo Una teoría que afirma que los procesos que le dan forma a la Tierra hoy en día, como la erosión y la sedimentación, también le dieron forma a la Tierra en el pasado; además, afirma que estos procesos ocasionan grandes cambios en tiempo geológico.

V

variable
Any factor that can change in a controlled experiment, observation, or model.

variable Cualquier factor que puede cambiar en un experimento controlado, en una observación o en un modelo.

vascular system (VAS-kyuh-lur)
Long tubelike tissues in plants through which water and nutrients move from one part of the plant to another. (p. 106)

sistema vascular Tejidos largos en forma de tubo en las plantas a través de los cuales se mueven agua y nutrientes de una parte de la planta a otra.

vegetative propagation
A form of asexual reproduction in plants, in which off-spring are produced from non-reproductive tissues such as leaves, stems, and roots. (p. 121)

propagación vegetativa Una forma de reproducción asexual en las plantas, en la cual las crías son producidas de tejidos no productivos tales como hojas, y raíces.

vein
A blood vessel that carries blood back to the heart. (p. 151)

vena Un vaso sanguíneo que lleva la sangre de regreso al corazón.

vertebrate
An animal with an internal backbone. (p. 97)

vertebrado Un animal que tiene columna vertebral interna.

vestigial organ (veh-STIHJ-ee-uhl)
A physical structure that was fully developed and functional in an earlier group of organisms but is reduced and unused in later species. (p. 83)

órgano vestigial Una estructura física que fue completamente desarrollada y funcional en un grupo anterior de organismos pero que está reducido y en desuso en especies posteriores.

volume
An amount of three-dimensional space, often used to describe the space that an object takes up.

volumen Una cantidad de espacio tridimensional; a menudo se usa este término para describir el espacio que ocupa un objeto.

W, X, Y

wave
A disturbance that transfers energy from one place to another without requiring matter to move the entire distance. (p. 160)

onda Una perturbación que transfiere energía de un lugar a otro sin que sea necesario que la materia se mueva toda la distancia.

wavelength
The distance from one wave crest to the next crest; the distance from any part of one wave to the identical part of the next wave. (p. 161)

longitud de onda La distancia de una cresta de onda a la siguiente cresta; la distancia de cualquier parte de una onda a la parte idéntica de la siguiente onda.

Z

zygote
A fertilized egg formed by the union of an egg cell and a sperm cell; a zygote can develop into a mature individual. (p. 119)

cigota Un huevo fertilizado formado por la unión de la célula de un huevo y una célula de esperma; una cigota se puede desarrollar hasta convertirse en un individuo maduro.

Acknowledgments

Photography

Cover, Title Page © Corbis; 3 top right © Stockbyte; 4 left © Getty Images; 5 © Getty Images; 10 right © Getty Images; 12 right © Getty Images; 16 © Rubberball Productions; 21 © Getty Images; 22 © Royalty-Free/Corbis; 23 © Getty Images; 24 © Getty Images; 25 © Getty Images; 34 © Getty Images; 40 top © Getty Images; 44 © Getty Images; 46 © Getty Images; 63 © Getty Images; 65 © Getty Images; 66 © Ismael Montero Verdu/ShutterStock; 70 © Chung Ooi Tan/ShutterStock; 73 left © D. Van Ravenswaay/Photo Researchers, Inc.; right © D. Van Ravenswaay/ Photo Researchers, Inc.; 74 Photograph by Aaron Shimer; 78 © Getty Images; 79 © Getty Images; 84 top Laurie O'Keefe; bottom left © Getty Images; bottom right © Getty Images; 88 © Photodisc/Getty Images; 89 © Getty Images; 91 left © Corbis; center © Getty Images; right © Getty Images; 96 © Getty Images; 97 © Getty Images; 98 top © Getty Images; center © Paul Whitted/ShutterStock; 99 © Getty Images; 108 © Getty Images; 122 bottom © mypokcik/ShutterStock; 148 © Pekka Jaakkola/ShutterStock; 150 © Artville; 162 © Getty Images; 174 © Gregory James Van Raalte/ShutterStock; 175 © Getty Images; 179 © Getty Images; 189 NASA/Lunar and Planetary Institute.

Illustrations and Maps

All maps, locators and globe locators by Geonova LLC, unless otherwise indicated.
Illustration by Argosy 161
Illustration by Peter Bull 6, 7, 103, 112, 125, 126
Illustration by Steve Cowden 167
Illustration by Myriam Kirkman-Oh/KO Studios 55 right, 106
Illustrations by Steve Oh/KO Studios 55 left and center
Illustration by Debbie Maizels 123, 136, 178
Illustration by Alan Male 72, 82
Illustration by Linda Nye 127, 128, 151, 153
Illustration by Dan Stuckenschneider/Uhl Studios 139, 140, 173, 188, 190
Illustration by Bart Vallecoccia 22, 24, 132, 149, 152, 155, 156, 163, 164, 191, 192, 193
Illustration by Jane Watkins 104
Illustration by Ian Jackson/Wildlife Art Ltd. 83,
Illustration by Mick Posen/Wildlife Art Ltd. 48, 49, 50, 88
Illustration by Peter Scott/Wildlife Art Ltd. 75
Illustration by Rob Wood 59
All other illustrations by McDougal Littell/Houghton Mifflin Co.